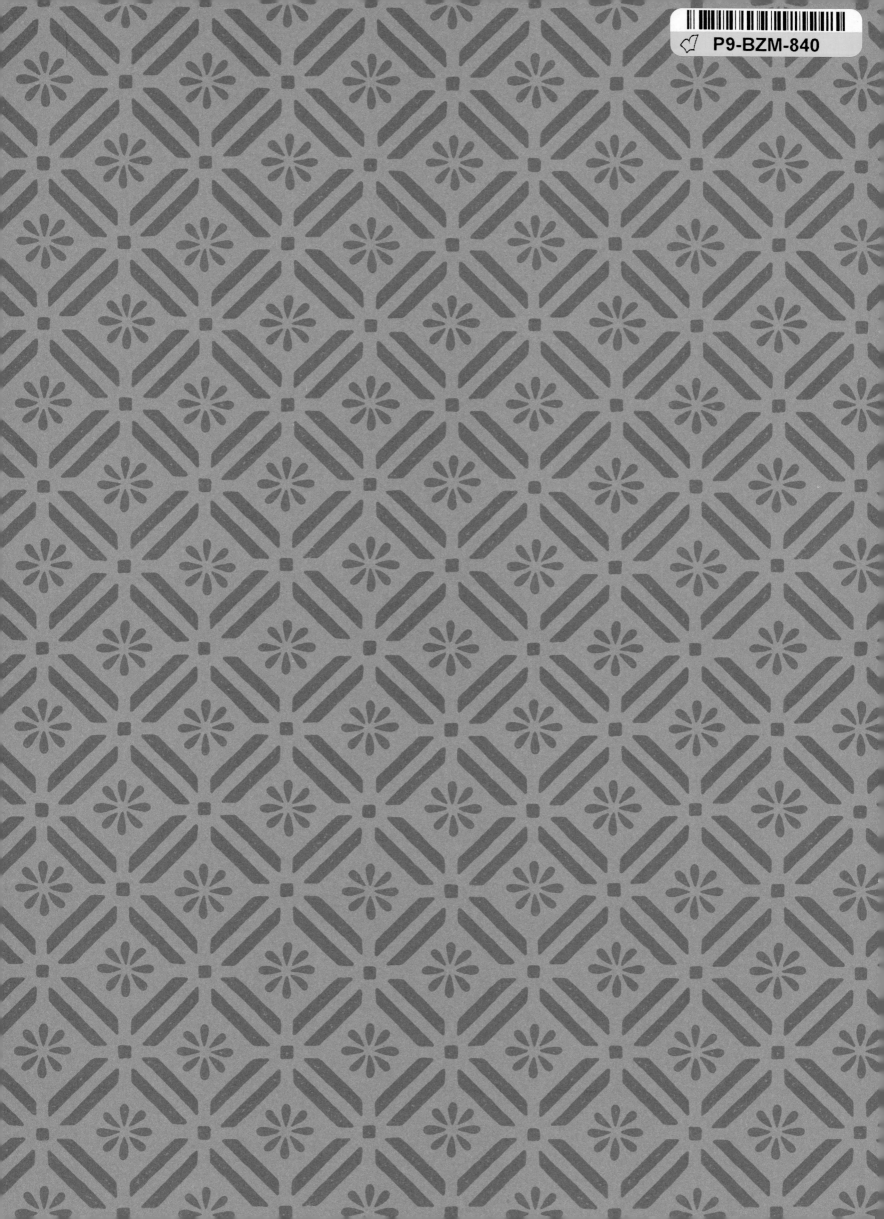

English House Style

John Goodall

English House Style

From the Archives
of *Country Life*

A VIEW THROUGH THE FRONT DOOR of Biddesden House, Wiltshire, taken in the summer of 1937. The house was built after 1710 by General John Richard Webb, a commander under the Duke of Marlborough and an MP. The hall is a lofty interior, two stories high, and has a chequerboard of stone and marble on the floor. This hard-wearing surface reflects the conventional role of the hall as an entrance space connecting the house to the outdoors. Here the relationship is underlined visually by the views through the windows. As is typical in eighteenth-century halls, the chairs are placed against the wall. The chain of the central lamp accentuates the height of the space. A huge portrait of the general on a horse presides over this space from the wall behind the camera.

Introduction

WHAT CAN IT POSSIBLY MEAN TO SAY THAT SOMETHING IS GOTHIC OR Classical? Both terms were invented centuries after the two styles they describe first came into existence, making them implicitly anachronistic and subjective. They are also hopelessly vague, since they could fairly accurately describe buildings or interiors of vastly different date, scale, purpose, character, and appearance. As if these difficulties weren't enough, styles are rarely pure; rather, they tend to mix themselves in bewildering ways. That's particularly true in a historic house, where a room many centuries old might contain striking modern objects, from television sets and furniture to paintings and light fixtures.

Yet for all the limitations associated with applying style labels, they remain impossible to escape. That's because references to style in casual discourse remain the only ways in which most of us—professionals and amateurs alike—can characterize or describe what we see. In such dialogue, stylistic labels are rarely applied with precision. Instead, they are allusive and live to an extent in the eye of the beholder. They are, in other words, useful rather than truthful things, and they should be recognized as such. This book attempts to use style labels as a point of departure to explore and characterize English interiors on a grand scale.

In this task it assumes an exceedingly broad canvas, covering interiors dating from the last 1,300 years. This depth of coverage may come as a surprise, but the reality is that not only do medieval interiors survive in quantity to this day (though many authorities ignore this fact), they also form an important foundation to the narrative. That's partly because the aesthetics and conventions of domestic use that informed the decoration of the medieval house cast very long shadows indeed. It's also because, contrary to what is generally implied in the structure of books on the subject, styles do not simply succeed one another in chronological order, one after the other. Rather, all of the most important styles have at least two lives: first as living traditions and then as conscious revivals. In some cases, such as the Gothic, its origin and subsequent revivals are relatively distinct, but that is often not the case.

To accommodate this peculiarity, the backbone of this book is formed by chapters that describe the grand narrative of stylistic change from the medieval period to the present day. It would have been possible to fragment this narrative further, and in some cases even to use different labels—this is a cake that could be cut in myriad ways. Nevertheless, the divisions I have chosen will, I hope, make sense and speak for themselves. The interiors covered in each chapter are arranged in broadly chronological order of creation, so that this arc of evolution from tradition to revival is clear. In every case it ends with a house in the twenty-first century.

Interspersed among the style chapters are four chapters addressing a particular type of building or theme of decoration: the cottage, the interest in the exotic, the home of the collector, and the garden room. To ensure a maximum breadth of coverage, individual houses appear only once in any given chapter. There are short introductions to every chapter that set out the historical background to each style or theme, but the real meat of the book lies in its photographs. For this reason, each image is accompanied by an extended caption that describes to the reader what they are seeing.

In the selection of images, I have taken pains to incorporate the work of as many architects and designers and possible, both celebrated and unfamiliar. Yet, whereas most books on interior design focus on the professionals involved and the character of their individual work, here the emphasis is slightly different. By definition, historic interiors are not blank canvases that can be freely reimagined. Architects and designers who work successfully with them must accommodate to existing structures and, ideally, improve upon them. This is an extremely

THE BOOT ROOM of Glenthorne, Devon. On whatever scale it is lived, the ideal of English country life is bound up with the outdoors.

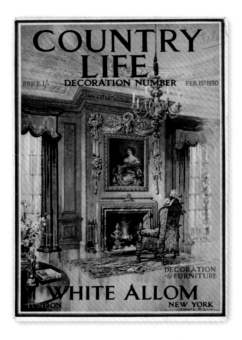

COUNTRY LIFE
PRICE 1/-   DECORATION NUMBER   FEB. 15 1930

DECORATION & FURNITURE

WHITE ALLOM
LONDON   NEW YORK

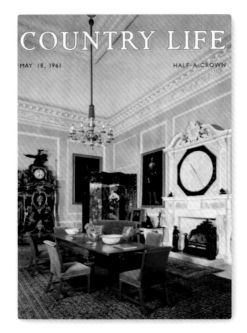

COUNTRY LIFE
MAY 18, 1961   HALF-A-CROWN

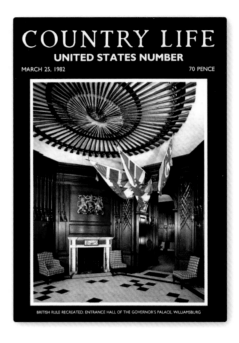

COUNTRY LIFE
UNITED STATES NUMBER
MARCH 25, 1982   70 PENCE

BRITISH RULE RECREATED: ENTRANCE HALL OF THE GOVERNOR'S PALACE, WILLIAMSBURG

COUNTRY LIFE
October 25, 1990 £1.50

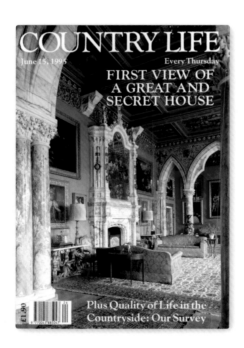

COUNTRY LIFE
June 15, 1995   Every Thursday

**FIRST VIEW OF
A GREAT AND
SECRET HOUSE**

Plus Quality of Life in the
Countryside: Our Survey

COUNTRY LIFE
FEBRUARY 29, 1996   EVERY THURSDAY £2

STARS OF THE STUD:
Britain's record-breaking supersires
Plus Stowe's romance restored
and a guide to the Cheltenham Festival

COUNTRY LIFE
SEPTEMBER 26, 1996   EVERY THURSDAY £2

**INTERIOR
DECORATION**

Plus
Tony Blair's
rural values:
an exclusive
interview

COUNTRY LIFE
SEPTEMBER 20, 2001   EVERY THURSDAY £2.60

INTERIOR DESIGN

PLUS
Lady Cranbrook's international
vegetable garden
The secret world
of British coral reefs
Young, fit
and fashionable:
beaters on grouse
shoots today

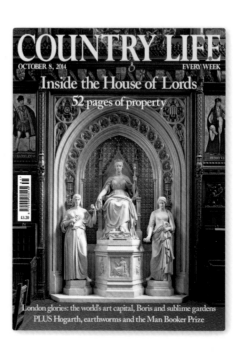

COUNTRY LIFE
OCTOBER 8, 2014   EVERY WEEK

Inside the House of Lords
52 pages of property

London glories: the world's art capital, Boris and sublime gardens
PLUS Hogarth, earthworms and the Man Booker Prize

challenging endeavor, and it places the contemporary professional in a collaboration with his or her predecessors.

All of the photographs in the book come from the peerless archive of *Country Life*. Built up week by week since the publication of the first issue in 1897, the archive offers an unparalleled insight into the changing face of grand domestic life in Britain over the last 120 years. And it continues to grow. Preserved within it are among the best photographs ever taken of the nation's most celebrated buildings, as well as those that are less familiar and even unknown. Indeed, the reach of the magazine into private properties, many of them completely inaccessible to the general public, is unrivaled. Famously, the archive is particularly strong in its coverage of country houses, but it does include a great deal more as the following pages illustrate.

About a third of the photographs featured here have never been published before, and the vast majority have been taken over the last decade while I have been architectural editor of the magazine. In that time I have worked with three photographers whose work is well represented here—the late Paul Barker (who died in 2016), Paul Highnam, and Will Pryce. Readers can judge for themselves what might otherwise sound like an extravagant claim: in various ways the work of these three photographers, and others represented, not only lives up to the highest standards of historic architectural photography, it outshines that of their contemporaries in the field.

Beyond the exceptional quality of its photography, one of the great advantages of the archive is that its photographs can usually be accurately dated. Also, it makes possible the illustration of rooms in their historic form, either when they were first created or before they were redecorated or demolished. For this reason, each chapter contains a handful of historic images in black and white.

The *Country Life* archive enjoys a particular important advantage of perspective in the twenty-first century. Because the weekly was founded when the British Isles were unified as one political entity, the national and regional borders that have subsequently sprung up in Ireland, Scotland, and Wales have never interfered with the magazine's oversight of what remains a common cultural inheritance. So, while this book focuses on interiors in England, it incorporates a selection of houses in Wales, Scotland, and Ireland that illustrate, or refract, trends apparent in English mainstream fashion.

It should also be noted that the images are not limited to domestic interiors. That's because, at different moments, public buildings such as theaters, clubs, assembly rooms, and even churches have all played an important role in formulating domestic taste. Indeed, before the age of the motorcar, few buildings outside London—the seat of fashion—were heavily visited. Most people learned about taste from their neighbors, from the buildings where they socialized, or from published images.

The reader might wonder what, if any, threads run through the chapters, drawing these interiors together? Is there an overarching English style, per se? The way the wealthy have lived in England is, of course, a particular product of the kingdom's unique social and political history. And that history, which is broadly outlined in the chapter introductions, does underpin some distinctive English traits, but I would say none can claim to be transcendent or unchanging.

Yet, as someone who visits large numbers of country houses, I am struck by one quality that, if it is not uniquely British, nevertheless does seem both distinctive and noteworthy: it's that so many of these homes accommodate a particular lifestyle associated with the outdoors—of dogs and horses, of muddy boots and riding crops. The result is that grand architecture and objects of great beauty are often mixed informally with the prosaic and the practical. In this mix, English country houses become homes as well.

Lastly, I'd like to emphasize that this book is very much a personal account. Just as two people might see totally different points of physical similarity among the faces they encounter on a crowded London bus, so might different eyes see in the houses and styles collected here quite different points of interest or emphasis. They might also prefer to assign to them different style labels. Indeed, quixotically, in some ways I hope they do. That's because this book is not written in the belief that these styles have some implicit integrity or meaning. Rather, they have helped me to characterize what I see and then to look further. I hope this book inspires the reader to do the same.

A SELECTION OF *COUNTRY LIFE* covers. The magazine has been charting the changing face of the domestic interior in Britain and beyond since 1897. Its first color photograph cover was, ironically, an image of the Lincoln Memorial in Washington, DC, that was published to mark the entry of America into World War I in 1917.

1

Romanesque

EVER SINCE THE DEPARTURE OF THE ROMANS IN THE EARLY fifth century, there have been recurrent bursts of interest in recreating the forms and splendor of Roman monumental architecture in Britain. What has lent that common endeavor such variety over the last millennium and a half is the radically different ways in which consecutive generations have understood the Roman world, as well as the vestiges of it that they found to copy.

The Romanesque style is a product of its first revival in the Middle Ages. It's characterized by massive stone construction, rich surface decoration, and the structural use of arches. It was sufficiently distinctive to inspire many subsequent imitations through the centuries. However, those who imitated the Romanesque prior to the late nineteenth century knew very little about it in historical terms. They simply saw in it a style that was ancient and British but not Classical. Consequently—and confusingly—they referred to the style by a wide variety of names, including Saxon and even Celtic.

Around the year 700 AD, the physical evidence of Roman occupation of Britain was much more prominent and ubiquitous than it is today. Even as ruins, Roman buildings were the largest man-made structures in the landscape. They were, moreover, much younger and correspondingly impressive. At that time, many major settlements, including London and York, still huddled within the embrace of Roman-built walls, and the network of roads that connected them was mostly constructed by the Romans.

These vestiges of Roman occupation were not only distinctive for their ubiquity and scale. They were also constructed from the most durable of materials—stone. The ability to cut thousands of blocks of this unyielding material, to move them to a building site, and order them into architecture was almost entirely beyond the technical means of Anglo-Saxon society. As a result they constructed most buildings, including all domestic buildings, of timber or other relatively ephemeral materials.

Occasionally, however, Anglo-Saxon builders aspired to permanence. Their most important ecclesiastical buildings were erected in stone. These spectacularly expensive endeavors, which grew markedly in ambition from about the year 1000, often recycled stone from Roman ruins and emulated their architectural forms, especially the arch, which was used to create wall openings and vaults. They were also modular in the sense that they used repeated elements, or bays, defined in elevation by strips of stone, shafts, or columns. Such buildings are termed Romanesque, after their source of inspiration.

It was an added appeal that the material of stone underlined the connection of Romanesque buildings with the papacy (and Rome). Pope Gregory the Great sent the first monks from Rome to convert the pagan Anglo-Saxons to Christianity in 597, but it was not until the Synod of Whitby in 664 that all kingdoms of England officially accepted the authority of the Roman Church. Consequently, and for all the difficulty of traveling to this distant city, Rome was not an unfamiliar place to the English. Its churchmen in particular returned from it laden with relics, art, books, memories of its architecture, and even specialists, such as one Abbot John, the chief cantor of St. Peter's, who came to England to teach the monks of Wearmouth, Northumberland, how to sing in 675.

The Norman Conquest of England in 1066 introduced new currents of influence in the revival of Roman architecture. With the wealth and power they seized, the new rulers of the kingdom—nearly all of them foreigners, with strange names, speaking an unfamiliar language and dressed in outlandish clothes—set about building on a monumental scale. They erected churches, founded new monasteries, constructed castles, and established towns.

Underpinning this herculean task was a command of the resources and technology necessary to quarry, work, and move stone on an unprecedented scale. Bound up with it from about 1090 was a fascination with the idea of encrusting the stone with abstract decorative carving. This may have been borrowed from the old Anglo-Saxon tradition of building with timber, though little is known about this today.

In the late twelfth century England became fascinated by a new aesthetic, what we now call Gothic. Yet even as artistic tastes moved on, the kingdom could not escape the legacy of the Romanesque. By virtue of their sheer scale, its buildings established the measure by which monumental architecture of the future would be judged. Constructed of stone, they also proved remarkably durable. Romanesque architecture lasted so well, indeed, that many of the castles and churches built in the eleventh and twelfth centuries far outlasted the memory of those who built them. By the sixteenth century, the greatest early medieval castles became associated with the foundation myths of the areas they dominated. The late twelfth-century castle keep of Kenilworth, for example, became the palace of Kenelm, a fictional king of a Middle English kingdom; eleventh-century Windsor Castle, built by William the Conqueror, was associated with King Arthur; and the Tower of London—also begun by William the Conqueror around 1072—was identified as a treasury built by Julius Caesar in 54 BC.

Such associations remained popularly accepted even into the nineteenth century. They gave the Romanesque style special status, for its rugged forms were suggestive of the strength necessary to lift the nation out of the chaos brought about by the collapse of Roman power. It became, in effect, Britain's foundational style. One surprising result of this association was that it was adopted for some theatrical sets connected with plays in the uncertain past, such as Shakespeare's *Macbeth*.

The Romanesque style became popular for prisons and courtrooms in the nineteenth century. Many architects of this time also worked on the restoration of medieval Romanesque churches, which introduced them to the complexities and sophistication of the style. In the twentieth and twenty-first centuries, the appeal of monumentality has waned, but the interest in certain Romanesque qualities, redolent of history, has unquestionably persisted.

THE HEAD OF THE MAIN STAIR of Penrhyn Castle in North Wales, rebuilt by the Regency architect Thomas Hopper between 1821 and 1833. The opulent decoration that encrusts every surface and feature is informed by a detailed knowledge of both Romanesque architectural and manuscript sources.

left

THE LATE SEVENTH-CENTURY CRYPT of Hexham Abbey, Northumberland, part of a church that was built by Wilfrid, Bishop of York, in about 674. It is constructed of stone pillaged from Roman buildings along Hadrian's Wall. Wilfrid knew Rome well and this interior was probably intended to evoke the catacombs there. This space may look barren to modern eyes, but it astonished churchgoers in the late seventeenth century: "My poor mind is at a loss for words to describe it" wrote one. " ... The crypt of beautifully dressed stone, the vast [church] structure ... with numerous side aisles ... winding passages and spiral staircases ... we have never heard of its like this side of the Alps." Here Northumbrian pilgrims could experience Rome. More than 1,300 years old, it's one of Britain's most ancient surviving interiors.

below left

THIS VAULTED CHAMBER AT DURHAM Castle—almost certainly a chapel—was probably completed by 1093, in the violent years that immediately followed the Norman Conquest of England. It is built entirely out of stone with a vault supported on six columns, a design apparently borrowed from contemporary Romanesque architecture on the Continent. Each column is crowned by a capital carved with scrolls at the corners. Both the columns and the capitals are drawn from Roman example. While the latter may look crude, they compare quite closely to Roman originals found in northern Britain, at the edge of the empire. The floor, with its neat parquet of stone slabs, is almost entirely original.

opposite

PRODUCING FOOD FOR A GREAT medieval country house on a daily basis was practically an industrial undertaking. The enormous kitchen of Raby Castle, Co. Durham, probably designed in the 1370s by the mason John Lewyn, would have been operated by a large staff divided into specialist teams (much as in a modern commercial kitchen). This ruggedly constructed building reflects the persistence of Romanesque techniques of construction into the late Middle Ages. Here, for example, the walls are sufficiently thick to accommodate an internal passage (partially visible beneath the window), a feature first found in grand Romanesque interiors. In a medieval household, it was typical for the servants to sleep in the same room they worked in, so the passage likely functioned as a sleeping area. The kitchen remained in use until the nineteenth century, hence the present fittings, painted in estate colors, and the copper pots.

below

THE GREAT HALL OF OAKHAM CASTLE, RUTLAND, was constructed about 1180–90. Most domestic buildings in this period were of wood, so this interior of stone is a rare survivor. The hall was the main domestic space within the castle fortifications, but probably also served as a courtroom (in which use it survived until the twentieth century). The custom, dating back to the Middle Ages, that celebrated visitors present a horseshoe upon their arrival at the place is the origin of the extraordinary collection hanging on the walls. As public buildings, halls were often spaces where family heirlooms, tapestries, and coats of arms were displayed. The interior preserves traces of decorative plaster imitating masonry patterns, a treatment copied from Roman buildings.

right

THE KEEP OR GREAT TOWER OF HEDINGHAM Castle, Essex, was built around 1140 and rises about one hundred feet, the benchmark height of a medieval skyscraper. This second floor chamber is the grandest in the building and is spanned by one of the largest medieval arches in England, a clear mark of the building's extraordinary ambition. The room was warmed by a large fire and may have possessed a painted ceiling. There is no specific evidence as to how this room was used in the twelfth century, but it was presumably a setting for ceremonies. If so, it is intriguing that the gallery running round the upper story is entered through a door carved with decoration only on one side. This may imply a correct way of entering and walking round the room.

above

FORDE ABBEY WAS AN IMPORTANT
Cistercian monastery that was converted
to domestic use at the Reformation. Its
buildings were further remodeled in the
1650s by Edmund Prideaux, a Puritan lawyer
who grew rich on the management of the
postal service during the Commonwealth.
Curiously, he preserved some of the
medieval monastic interiors, including this
fine twelfth-century chamber, the chapter
house, which became a household chapel.
His principal addition was the screen and
wainscoting around the walls, which was
added for warmth. The austere Classical
detailing of the seventeenth-century
woodwork echoes that of the interior's
Romanesque architecture.

opposite

THIS DOOR IS THE ENTRANCE TO THE
great hall of Eastnor Castle, Herefordshire,
begun in 1812 by Lord Somers. The building,
designed on a magnificent scale by the
architect Robert Smirke, combined the
medieval trappings of fortification with
every modern convenience. Smirke was
recommended to Lord Somers by Lord
Lowther, the creator of another vast house in
the castellated style at Lowther in Cumbria.
This hall rises through the heart of the
building and was virtually devoid of internal
ornament. The decoration and wall painting
around the door were late nineteenth-
century additions in a Neo-Byzantine
idiom—another Neo-Roman style—by
the Norwich-born designer and architect
G. E. Fox. They add color and liveliness to
this cavernous space.

above

THE HALL OF ADARE MANOR,
Co. Limerick, was created in about 1840.
It is entered through doors covered in gilded
Spanish leatherwork, doubtless purchases
made by the Earl of Dunraven during his
European travels with his wife in the 1830s.
They hang in a magnificent Romanesque
archway, one of several in the room that
are carved from polished grey marble and
inspired by Irish medieval examples. The
integration of abstract sculpture within
architecture, as shown here in the treatment
of the doorway arches, was one of the most
important legacies of the Romanesque.
This photograph was taken in 1969.

opposite

THE MAIN HALL OF PENRHYN CASTLE,
part of a vast castle in the Romanesque
style erected between 1821 and 1833 by the
architect Thomas Hopper. The marvelously
rich surface decoration was created using
a combination of stone carving and plaster.
The detailing is accurately, if eclectically,
drawn from medieval precedents. Much of
Hopper's knowledge of medieval architecture
evidently came from books and articles,
themselves evidence of a burgeoning interest
in the antiquarian study of the Middle Ages
at the time. Despite such study, the dating
of medieval architecture remained poorly
understood at the time: this style was often
described as Saxon and was mistakenly
believed to date from the period immediately
following the collapse of the Roman empire.

previous pages

THE VAULTED DRAWING ROOM ON
the ground floor of Lambay Castle in Dublin
Bay might easily be mistaken for a medieval
interior. With massive walls, semicircular
arches, and vaulting it is essentially
Romanesque in character. The castle was
built in the sixteenth century and adapted
by the architect Edwin Lutyens from 1908.
Lutyens extended the castle for Cecil
Baring and his wife, Maude, the youngest
daughter of the American millionaire and
tobacco manufacturer Pierre Lorillard.
The architectural detailing of the interior,
including the semicircular arch of the vault,
is articulated with blue-grey stone from
Milverton on the mainland. This color is
echoed in the upholstery of the chairs.

above

FROM 1919 THE ARCHITECT RANDALL
Wells took over responsibility for alterations
to Wardington Manor, Oxfordshire. Two
years previously he had married the
divorced Molly Waters, a society beauty
with a passionate interest in the arts. She
had briefly run the Guild of St. Veronica,
which promoted crafts such as bookbinding,
leatherwork, and embroidery by women.
It seems that she is responsible for the
remarkable decorative plasterwork that
extends across the walls and ceilings of
several rooms in this house. Here the design
is like Romanesque zig-zag, or chevron.
Serpents weave through an arcade at the
head of the wall and acrobats perform in the
window sill.

opposite

THE CORRIDOR LINKING THE HALL
and dining room at Cour House, Kintyre,
was built in 1920–22 for the ship insurance
broker John Braidwood Gray. Visible to
the right is the foot of the main staircase.
Cour was the first major commission of
Oliver Hill, an architect much favored by
Country Life. With its massive walls and
boldly chamfered arches, the interior is
Romanesque in character. Its rendered
surfaces, however, are redolent of the Arts
and Crafts love of texture and materials. The
interior is unusually broad in relation to its
height, an effect emphasized by the low-
springing of the arches. Hill spent time in
a shepherd's hut to understand this remote
site before he began to design the house.

THE NINETEENTH-CENTURY
dining room of the Old Rectory at
Quenington, Gloucestershire, is
today a playful Neo-Romanesque
interior furnished with
contemporary furniture. It has been
created by David and Lucy Abel
Smith, who have lived here since the
1980s. The cycle of frescoes, which
are deliberately fragmentary, was
painted by Neil Mackay and depicts
the lives of the saints David and
Lucy. Incorporated in the design
is architectural detailing inspired
by that in the neighboring twelfth-
century parish church of St. Swithin.
A cloister is depicted through the
archway. The table is by Fred Baier,
its form and coloring inspired by the
idiosyncratic work of the nineteenth-
century architect William Burges.
Each chair has animal finials added
by Lucy Strachan and a distinct
fabric cover by Alexandra Lacey.

right

A TWENTY-FIRST-CENTURY ROMANESQUE screen made of oak in the former lodging of the prior of Wenlock, now known as Wenlock Abbey, Shropshire. The lodging, which today is a private house, stands beside the ruins of a Cluniac monastery that was suppressed during the Reformation. Oak for the screen was selected by the carpenter Bernard Allen from the nearby Powis Castle estate, and its sculptural reliefs were carved by Andrew Pearson. The reliefs themselves were designed by the owner of the house, the artist Louis de Wet, and depict scenes from his life. The screen took fifteen years to make. De Wet also designed a Romanesque library with oak bookshelves in the room above the one shown here, which was inspired by depictions of the *studiolo* of St. Jerome, such as *Saint Jerome in His Study* by Albrecht Dürer.

following pages

IN 2009 ENGLISH HERITAGE, THEN a state-funded body managing hundreds of historic buildings in state care, decorated the keep, or great tower, of Dover Castle as it might have looked during a visit by King Henry II in 1184. The aim was to provide an exacting recreation of a twelfth-century interior based on existing source material, including manuscript illustrations. All the furniture is painted, including the bed, which is the centerpiece of the room. It is from beds and their canopies that thrones, overhung by canopies, later developed. Kings and noblemen traveled constantly in the Middle Ages, and their possessions— expressions of their wealth—were carried from place to place with them. Thus, like the stage of a theater, rooms were dressed only when they were occupied.

Gothic

THE TERM *GOTHIC* WAS FIRST USED IN THE SEVENTEENTH CENTURY to describe the architecture of the Middle Ages. Confusingly, however, at the moment it came into common use, the subject of medieval architecture and its evolution was poorly understood. As a result, almost anything ancient, vaulted, and stone-built might be described by the term. Nor was there consensus about the formal development of such buildings, or even which were created in the Middle Ages, as opposed to the more ancient Roman past, or Dark Ages. Only by slow degrees did the pointed arch—what is now universally understood to be the mark of the Gothic style—come to be recognized as the defining feature of this style.

During the early eighteenth century, the first attempts were made to study English medieval architecture (the Society of Antiquaries was founded in 1707). At the same time, the Gothic began to be associated with English political tradition and to express the liberties enshrined in the Magna Carta of 1215. It's no coincidence, therefore, that one of the first secular commissions in the Gothic style was explicitly associated with government: the 1739 screen inserted in the great hall of the eleventh-century Westminster Palace, the seat of the royal courts in London. Thereafter, through books and antiquarian study, interest in medieval architecture developed rapidly.

One of its most famous advocates was the dilettante Horace Walpole, whose celebrated house at Strawberry Hill, Twickenham, has lent its name to the exquisite style of eighteenth-century Gothic it embodies. Walpole personally presided over the design of this building, working with a circle of friends and cutting engravings of medieval monuments from books to serve as patterns for the craftsmen he employed. In his amusing and acerbic published correspondence, Walpole sometimes presented both his house and the Gothic style as a caprice. He was, perhaps, being disingenuous. The widespread use of Gothic in a domestic setting did have a serious purpose, as an expression both of ancestry (a long-standing obsession of gentry and aristocratic families) and of a new sensibility, Romanticism.

As the Gothic grew in popularity it became established as a stylistic counterpart to mainstream Classicism. It is, indeed, to the late eighteenth century that we owe the idea that the Gothic and Classical are styles at odds with one another. Whereas the Classical style is regular, symmetrical, and ordered, Gothic is unconstrained by rules of propriety and is appropriate, therefore, for fantastical designs and flights of fancy. Henceforth they became respectively established as the head and the heart of style.

Then, in the early nineteenth century, came the novels of Sir Walter Scott. It's difficult to overestimate the influence of books such as *Ivanhoe* (1820), which vividly evoked life in medieval Britain. This and other books fueled an enthusiasm for further investigation into the architecture of the Middle Ages and into its values and ideals. Of the latter, nothing proved more influential than the idea of chivalry, a code of behavior underpinned by an intoxicating mixture of love and religion.

All this coincided with the end of the Napoleonic Wars in 1815, a time when Britain was starting to emerge as the richest and most powerful nation in the world. Small surprise, then, that the coronation of George IV in 1821 saw the court dressed in Tudor-inspired finery and the arrival of the king's champion dressed in armor. Or that in 1839 huge crowds arrived in pouring rain to watch the flower of Britain's aristocracy disport itself in armor and medieval clothing at the Eglinton Tournament.

The moral purpose of this medieval revival infused the writing of perhaps the greatest revivalist of the Gothic, Augustus Welby Pugin. He formed part of a generation that examined the remains of Gothic building with great care and published them to a receptive public audience. His understanding of the style is perfectly expressed in the title of what is perhaps his most famous publication, *The True Principles of Pointed or Christian Architecture* (1841).

Pugin and his fellow Neo-Gothic practitioners, however, achieved something beyond merely the revival of an architectural style. Their interest in church design encouraged them to think in an integrated way about the decoration of the buildings they designed, including their glass, wallpapers, carpets, and furnishings. This decorative work was

THE GALLERY OF STRAWBERRY HILL, Twickenham, was created between 1761 and 1763 by one of the pioneers of the Gothic revival, Horace Walpole. The vault is directly copied from the Lady Chapel of Westminster Abbey, begun in 1503. The room displayed some of the finest pictures, marbles, bronzes, majolica, and Sèvres china in Walpole's collection.

executed to a very high standard and informed domestic decoration. Companies such as Morris & Co., established in 1861, emerged to feed the consequent demand for high quality furnishings.

Over the course of the nineteenth century, the British public became steadily more enamored of the Gothic style and the intricacies of its evolution. Moreover, through the eyes of figures such as the critic and writer John Ruskin, they began to see it in the context of European medieval architecture. At the same time, Gothic was reinvented as a completely modern style, appropriate for every type of building, from an almshouse to a railway station.

Gradually, the British fascination with the Gothic waned. This decline was in part due to the cycle of fashion. There was also, however, a more deeply imbedded distrust of the moral imperatives that underpinned the Gothic revival and mockery of its opulence and ecclecticism. By the early twentieth century, critics were beginning to present the whole episode as a disastrous mistake and looking back beyond it, fell in love with the eighteenth century and the idea of taste. The appeal of taste was that it seemed to imply that a building or interior could be judged on its aesthetic merits alone. It also allowed for a distinction to be made between revivals of Gothic that were morally and archaeologically informed (and disapproved of) and ones that were not (which might still be delightful). To underline the distinction, the latter were given a new name, "Gothick," the quaint spelling evoking its supposedly whimsical character.

After a period of almost complete rejection, the Gothic style enjoyed a slow revival during the late twentieth century. One of the greatest essays in the style in recent years has been the reconstruction of the state apartments at Windsor Castle after a fire in 1992. The success of the work at Windsor is partly connected to the history and associations of the building itself, but the project is also undeniably a spectacular modern reworking of the Gothic style.

THE CENTRAL STAIRCASE HALL OF Ashridge, Hertfordshire, designed by the architect James Wyatt and completed before his death in 1813. This huge house, whose service buildings ramble into the neighboring county of Buckinghamshire, was built on the site of a former monastery, and the sculpture in this vast internal space celebrates the personalities associated with this institution (see page 47).

above

THE GREAT CHAMBER AT LONGTHORPE Tower, Cambridgeshire, allows a modern visitor to imagine a luxurious English domestic interior of the early fourteenth century. It occupies the first floor of a tower built around 1300 by Robert Thorpe, one in a family dynasty of lawyers acting for Peterborough Abbey in Northamptonshire. As originally completed around 1330, the scheme was painted in vivid colors with details picked out in gilding. The lower register depicts a hanging cloth, possibly the backdrop to a chair or bed that dominated the room and would have stood close to the fireplace (invisible, to the left). The vault is painted with images of musicians. Above the door to the right is a painting of the Bonnacon, a legendary beast that threw flaming excrement at its pursuers. These paintings were discovered in 1945.

opposite

THE ORIEL WINDOW OF THE GREAT chamber at Great Chalfield Manor, Wiltshire, built in the late 1460s. Raised up a step from the floor level of the interior, brilliantly lit by a circle of windows, and covered with a splendid vault, this was a clearly demarcated space within the room. Great chambers were used for formal entertainment, and it is possible that the owner of the house might have withdrawn to this privileged area to speak privately with guests. The pendant vaults over the oriel hint at the sophisticated provenance of this building, which was designed by an unknown mason familiar with contemporary royal building projects. This detail is a precursor of the decorated plaster ceilings in the Tudor period.

following pages

THE CONVOCATION HOUSE, OXFORD, was built in the 1630s as a chamber of debate for the university. In an unbroken tradition from the Middle Ages to the seventeenth century, the universities of Oxford and Cambridge continued to build in the Gothic style, which was understood to express the history of these institutions with their deep roots in the medieval past. For the same reason, church architecture often used these forms as well. This chamber, with its benches, served as a parliament chamber on several occasions during the English Civil War of the1640s and brings us close to the physical intimacy of the House of Commons prior to its nineteenth-century reconstruction at Westminster.

below

THE GOTHIC HALL OF WELBECK ABBEY, Nottinghamshire, in a photograph published in 1906. This spectacular room was created by the dowager Countess of Oxford in 1751. Her interests in the Gothic style may have been shaped by her husband, Edward Harley, whose important manuscript collection—part of a huge library he amassed—helped establish the founding collection of the British Library. The pendant vaults are copied from Henry VII's chapel, Westminster Abbey, a building that has been consistently admired since its completion in the early sixteenth century. There is Gothic paneling around the lower register of the room. The interior is shown with a slightly incongruous overlay of Victorian plants, exotica, and bric-a-brac.

opposite

STRAWBERRY HILL, TWICKENHAM, was leased by Horace Walpole in 1747. He went on to develop it as a shrine to Gothic taste. Shown here is the chapel, also known as the Tribune or Cabinet, which he built in the 1760s and used to display elements of his superb collection of medieval curiosities. The decoration on the walls draws from the fourteenth-century tracery of York Minster's great west window. Walpole worked with a circle of friends—what he called his Committee of Taste—to develop his designs and cut out engravings from books to inform them. Walpole was obsessed by his reputation. If his correspondence had been less voluminous, less readable, or less quotable, his claim to have master-minded the Gothic revival would never have been taken seriously.

IN 1764 MILTON MANOR, OXFORDSHIRE, was purchased by Bryant Barrett, a wealthy Catholic who made a fortune manufacturing silver and gold brocade. He numbered the court and much of the nobility among his clients. With such cosmopolitan connections, it's small surprise that Barrett hired Stephen Wright, Deputy Surveyor of the Board of Works, to add two new wings to his seat. One of them incorporated a chapel and a library, shown here. It preserves its original bookcases and books, which were thoughtfully collected by Barrett. His choice of Gothic was undoubtedly inspired by his Catholicism. The treatment, however, is typical of the style as developed by William Kent in the mid-eighteenth century. Over the fireplace is a conversation piece showing Barrett and his first wife sitting beside a splendid gilded table, Barrett turning toward his wife as if about to address her. A spaniel lies at their feet.

opposite

THE EARLY SIXTEENTH-CENTURY
north cloister walk of Forde Abbey, Dorset,
survived the transformation of the medieval
monastic buildings into a house after the
Reformation. As originally completed
(or intended, because the interior may never
have been finished) the walk would have
been covered with an intricately detailed
fan vault. Around 1800, the present plaster
vaults were inserted on the springs of their
medieval predecessors. The large windows
of the medieval cloister give the space the
look of a conservatory. The combination
of medieval and Georgian fabric is
very satisfying.

above

SOON AFTER THE 11TH EARL OF
Pembroke inherited Wilton, Wiltshire, in
1794, he hired the architect James Wyatt to
re-order the building so as "to give a large
house the comfort and convenience of a
small one." He wanted the building "Wyatted
in good Gothick Taste," a style that seemed
particularly appropriate since Wilton had
been a nunnery before the Reformation.
Shown here is an upper walk of the two-story
cloister added in 1800–02 to help circulation
within the building. The lower cloister was
for servants. In recent years the collection of
Roman sculpture originally displayed here
has been returned. Wyatt's relationship with
the earl was soured by the architect's lack
of organization, outrageous bills, and the
structural failure of the cloister.

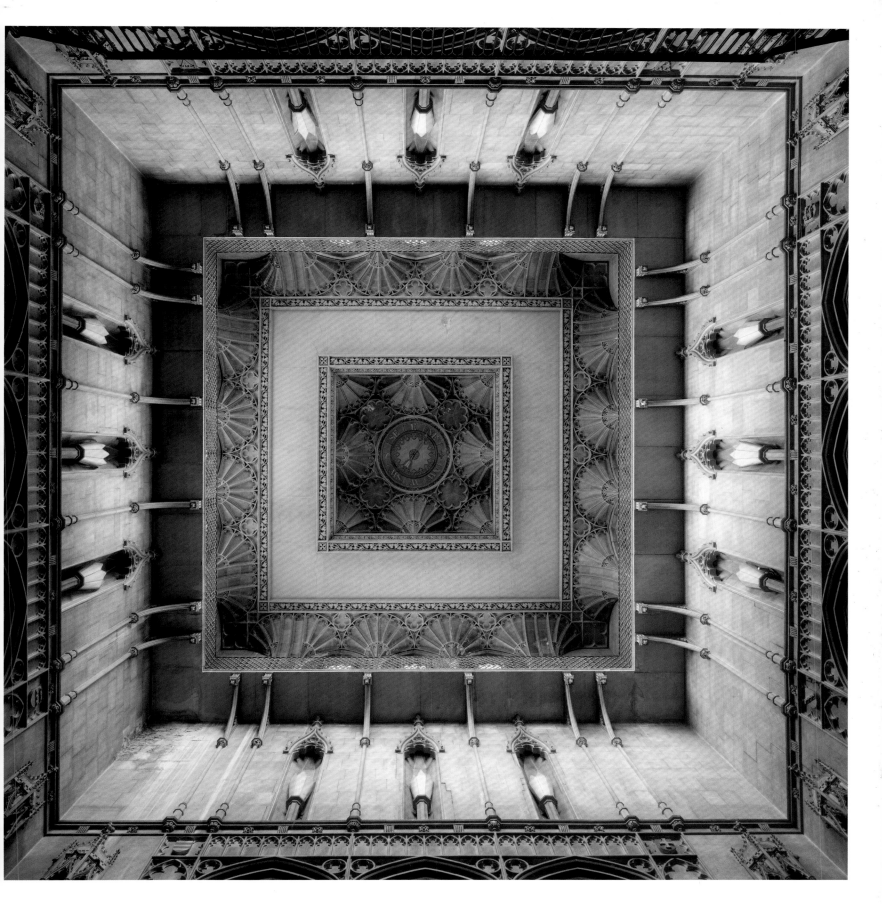

THE GALLERY OF CHARLEVILLE CASTLE, Co. Offaly, in Ireland, was built between 1800 and 1809 by Lord Charleville. In his guidebook to the house, he explained that the house aimed "to exhibit specimens of Gothic architecture, as collected from Cathedrals and Chapel-tombs, and to show how they may be apply'd to Chimney Pieces, Ceilings, windows, balustrades etc." It is, in fact, very eclectic in its borrowings of Gothic detail, most of them lifted from printed antiquarian volumes such as James Cavanah Murphy's

measured drawings of the Portuguese monastic church at Batalha. The house was also influenced by Horace Walpole's house at Strawberry Hill, which Lord Charleville visited with his wife in July 1802.

THE STUCCO FAN VAULT AND WIND VANE of the central tower of Ashridge House, Hertfordshire, designed by James Wyatt after 1808. This gigantic house was commissioned by the Duke of Bridgewater

on the site of a former medieval monastery. The duke was a high-church Tory landowner, who lavished money on improvements to his estate and its churches. According to his chaplain, the duke regarded the Gothic style as "recalling ... the devotion and austerity of the cloister, as well as the generous virtues of our ancient nobility." The main stair of the house overlooks the interior of the central tower. Incorporated in the stair decoration are sculptures of historical figures associated with the property.

THE 1820s ENTRANCE HALL OF Abbotsford, Roxburghshire, in Scotland was created by the Romantic novelist Sir Walter Scott as a showcase for his celebrated collection of antiquities. It was conceived in the image of the baronial halls he describes in his hugely popular novels *Ivanhoe* and *Rob Roy*. The hall was hung with armor and paneled using timber from the oak pews salvaged from Dunfermline Abbey. There is armorial glass in the windows and the roof paint was distressed so as to appear "somewhat weather beaten and faded." Local craftsmen, such as the joiner Joseph Shillinglaw and the Smiths of Darnick carried out the work under the direction of David Ramsay Hay, a friend of Scott and a fashionable Edinburgh designer.

above

FROM 1768 THE 2ND EARL OF DARLINGTON employed the prolific architect John Carr of York to remodel his seat, the rambling but magnificent medieval castle of Raby, Co. Durham. It was difficult for carriages to turn in the castle courtyard so in 1782 Carr created a carriage entrance within the lower part of the fourteenth-century hall range. To gain clearance for vehicles, he raised the ceiling of the hall, which he supported on two lines of columns. In 1815 the 3rd Earl had the columns clad in false marble, termed *scagliola*, which

greatly adds to the splendor of the room. From this covered entrance guests could ascend the far staircase, a feature planned by Carr but executed later to a slightly different design.

following pages

IN 1831 WILLIAM COURTENAY, A SON OF the Bishop of Exeter, successfully revived the earldom of Devon, which had fallen into abeyance in 1556, in his favor. Four years later he inherited the former seat of the earldom at Powderham, Devon, which he was

determined to improve as "an ancient castle." The architect Charles Fowler, who had been born at Cullompton in Devon and had made his name as the builder of covered markets, including Covent Garden, London, undertook the work and created this new entrance hall. Its form and heraldry celebrate the antiquity of the Courtenay line. The fireplace is a copy of the one in the bishop's palace at Exeter, which was commissioned by Peter Courtenay, Bishop of Exeter, in 1478. Presumably the earl remembered it from his childhood.

above left

TAYMOUTH CASTLE, PERTHSHIRE, is one of the most ambitious Gothic mansions in Britain. In its present form it is largely the creation of the Earl of Breadalbane, who began to expand it on an exponential scale in 1801. The Baronial Hall, shown here, was constructed by Archibald and James Elliot, who worked closely with the London plasterer and sculptor Francis Bernasconi. Their relatively austere original creation was then sumptuously enriched in preparation for a four-day visit by Queen Victoria and Prince Albert

in 1842. The figures responsible for this elaboration—including the fireplace, paneling, and painting visible here—were the architect James Gillespie Graham, who worked with A. W. N. Pugin, and the London decorating firm of Frederick Crace & Son. The chimneypiece is probably inspired by late-medieval bronze tomb grills of the early sixteenth century.

above right

THE DRAWING ROOM AT EASTNOR Castle, Herefordshire, was decorated from 1849 by J. G. Crace and A. W. N. Pugin. Eastnor was a Regency castle (begun in 1812) of the kind that Pugin, the evangelist of the Gothic revival, particularly hated. It seems, however, that Crace may have concealed the history of the building from his partner in London, who never visited. The most striking thing about the interior is its sumptuous polychromy. Over the fireplace is a family tree of the Somers family conceived by Pugin. The room has

been sensitively restored in recent years and was supplied in 2011 with a new carpet designed by Hazel Fox and Lucy Hervey-Bathurst of Lucy Manners Interiors. Its pattern is informed by Pugin's design for the lost original carpet in the Victoria and Albert Museum. The replacement was woven by Asad Carpets in Turkey.

following pages

THE HOUSE OF LORDS CHAMBER, completed in 1852, was rebuilt in the Gothic style following a disastrous fire in 1834. Charles Barry, the architect responsible, described this room as "not a mere place of business, nor even a mere House of Lords—but as a chamber in which a sovereign, surrounded by the court, summoned the three estates of the realm." The sovereign's throne is visible at the far end of the room, one of A. W. N. Pugin's most superb creations. Regal red and gold are the predominant colors of the interior (as opposed to green in the House of Commons). The interior decoration trumpets Britain's history. Supporting the ceiling, for example, are statues of the barons and bishops who secured the Magna Carta at Runnymede in 1215.

above

THE SUMMER SMOKING ROOM AT
Cardiff Castle, Glamorgan, is set within
a high tower. Completed in 1873, it
was designed by the architect William
Burges for the 3rd Marquess of Bute in a
magnificent Neo-Gothic style. This was a
male domain. A gilded candelabrum with
rays like the sun is suspended in the center
of the room and there is a gallery above it
from which smokers could enjoy the views.
Depicted in sculpture and tile around the
walls is a wealth of imagery including
Classical and biblical figures. The floor is
laid with tiles and beneath the table is a
brass map of the world. It bears a punning
inscription that describes the map—and by
implication the room—as a microcosm of
the world.

opposite

ST. PANCRAS STATION, LONDON, OPENED
originally in 1873. After a heroic restoration
campaign, the hotel that forms its principal
façade reopened its doors in 2011. The
Grand Stair, seen here, is the showpiece of
the hotel, and was designed by Sir George
Gilbert Scott. It connects the reception
rooms on the ground floor with the
bedrooms above. The stair is supported on
richly ornamented iron beams and rises and
divides on each floor. Over the whole is a
soaring Gothic vault. In the late nineteenth
century, railway travel around the world
created a new demand for hotels, many
of which, like this one, assumed palatial
proportions. Scott saw the possibilities of
Gothic as a modern style and developed its
forms to serve the industrial world.

opposite

THE ENTRANCE HALL OF HAYNE MANOR,
Devon, is a modern essay in Gothic design by
the architect Michael Brooke. It formed part
of a wider renovation of the building—which
includes a Gothic kitchen—undertaken
by the Earl and Countess of Stockton
following their purchase of the house in a
dilapidated state in 1994. The architect's
design was transformed into a ceiling by
Hayles and Howe of Bristol, with gilding by
Martin Hull. Working drawings were made
by Peter Dlugiewicz. The floor is of local
slate. Inspiration for the room came from
eighteenth-century Irish buildings.

above

THE WESTON TOWER AT WESTMINSTER
Abbey, London, was designed by Ptolemy
Dean Architects and opened in 2018. It's an
ingenious work of contextual architecture
that allows public access by stair and lift to
the Queen's Diamond Jubilee Galleries in
the upper gallery space, or triforium, of this
great thirteenth-century church. In plan the
tower takes the form of an eight-pointed star,
a device taken from medieval decoration in
the abbey. This geometry is legible even in the
framing of the ceiling and floor shown here.
The tower elevation evokes the multifaceted
or "compass" windows that are a distinctive
feature of late-medieval English architecture.
Through the windows, visitors can enjoy
close-up views of the abbey church.

THE GREAT HALL OF CROSBY HALL,
London, originally formed part of a house
called Crosby Place on Bishopsgate in the
City of London that was owned in the late
fifteenth century by the merchant prince
Sir John Crosby. In 1909–10 the hall he
created, which probably dates to about 1475,
was dismantled and transferred to Chelsea.
Preserved from the original structure is
this vaulted oriel window. The cobalt blue,
red, and gold of the oriel vault, as well as the
stained glass in the windows, are the work of
the present owner, Dr. Christopher Moran.
He bought the property in 1988 and has since
recreated Crosby Hall as a Thames-side
Tudor mansion.

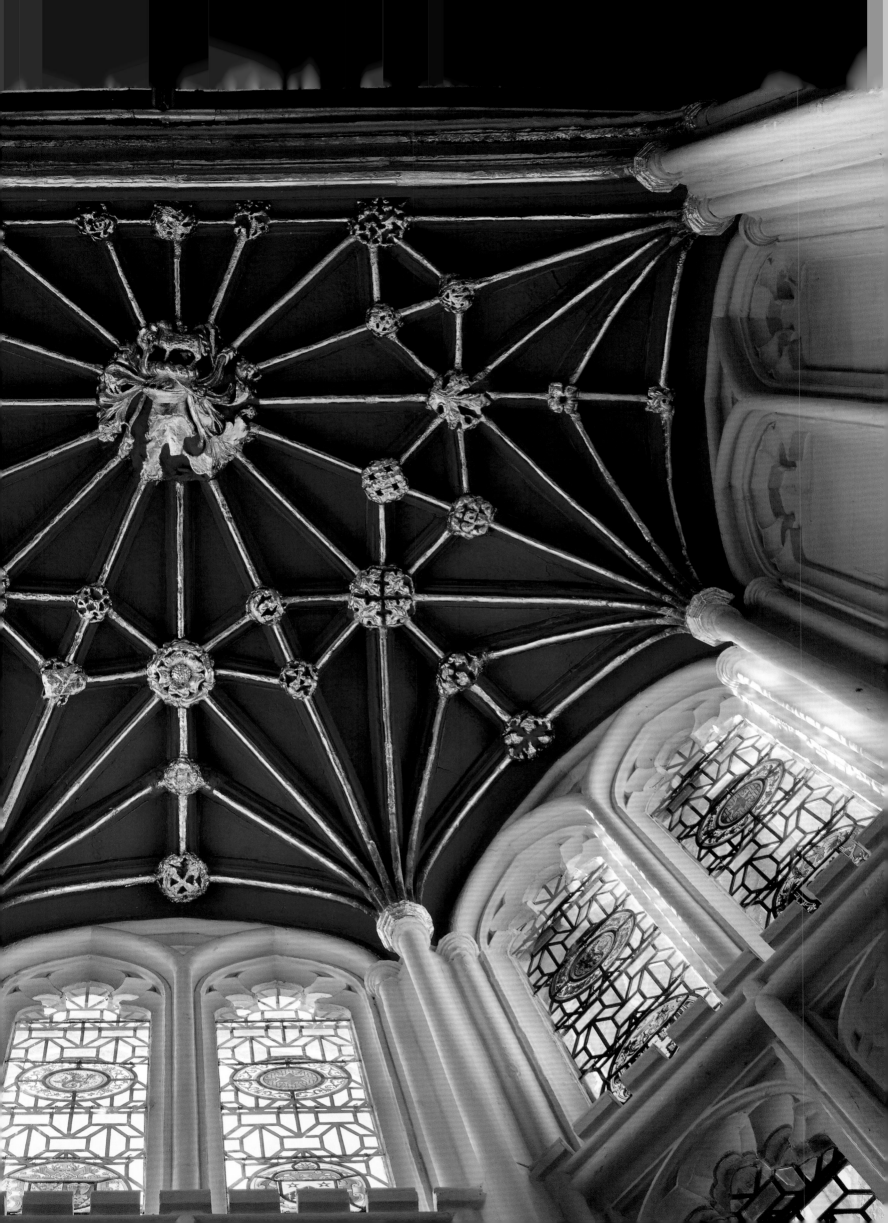

3

The Collector

ALL OF US COLLECT, BUT SOME OF US COLLECT MORE SERIOUSLY than others. And for the most serious collectors of all, houses—or at least particular rooms—become stage sets for the display of collections. Britain has a long and varied history of collecting, but it is only the tradition of assembling books, as well as the room that displays the collection, that has been sufficiently consistent across the centuries to win for itself a familiar name: the library.

Setting that aside, collecting is a pastime without an obvious beginning, and it is one that is entirely personal and idiosyncratic, but it does exhibit clear trends across the millenia. A medieval noble might have collected relics and had the finest set in superb mounts of goldsmith work; a descendent in the reign of Elizabeth I, natural curiosities, intaglios, or medals; a Stuart aristocrat, paintings, sculpture, or rare ceramics; a figure of the Enlightenment, specimens of fossils; a Victorian missionary, taxidermy specimens of exotic creatures from across the world; a wealthy country house owner in the twenty-first century, contemporary art, pottery, train sets, or even paperweights. In each case, the choice offers an insight into the mind and interests of the collector, as well as the changing character and outlook of the world they occupied.

The process of collection is implicitly one of learning and refinement. Each acquisition demands categorization, which in turn imposes a logic or aesthetic on its display and contextual arrangement. There are working collections in which the objects continue to function, for example, with clocks. Nevertheless, the very act of gathering artifacts or objects together sets them apart and elevates them above their original function; you don't need many clocks to know the time. In the process, collecting dignifies the selected objects; even the most trivial items can look impressive, even lovely, en masse.

Collections can present challenges for the viewer. Some demand high levels of understanding to interpret, or pure geekiness to appreciate. Whether weird or wonderful, all should offer something to marvel at, either for their intrinsic value, their associations, or as a curiosity. They also conjure questions about those who troubled to collect them, even when they seem familiar. What does it say, for example, of Sir William Gladstone, the nineteenth-century statesman and bibliophile, that his library at Hawarden Castle, Flintshire, in Wales is filled with logging axes from around the world?

previous pages
THE 1830s GOTHIC HOUSE AT Glenthorne, Devon, is filled with the collections of Sir Christopher Ondaatje. The contents of the library reflect his many interests, including literature, publishing, sculpture, and art from his native Sri Lanka. The frame in front of the door to the right, for example, displays a nineteenth-century wax model of a Sinhalese village scene.

opposite
THE PANTHEON AT INCE BLUNDELL HALL, Lancashire. The building is a copy of the Pantheon in Rome and was constructed in 1802–10 as a freestanding structure but was later joined to the adjacent house. In this photograph taken in 1958 it is shown with an eclectic array of sculpture amassed by Henry Blundell, a celebrated collector of Classical marbles. Blundell was inspired to collect by the example of his neighbor Charles Townley, another wealthy Catholic. Townley's collection, which was internationally celebrated, was purchased in 1805 by the British Museum. All the freestanding sculpture shown here is now in the possession of the Liverpool Museums. Only the sculptures fixed to the building and inside the niches and roundels remain in their original place. Hopefully one day this interior will be recreated as originally intended by Blundell.

above

THE VASE ROOM OF DEEPDENE, SURREY, photographed by *Country Life* in 1899. It displays the vase collection of the furniture designer Thomas Hope. This was previously displayed in Hope's London house and, along with his sculpture collection, enjoyed celebrity. Hope purchased Deepdene in 1807 and set about improving it by stages, using the architect William Atkinson to realize his ideas. Hope was influential through his writings, notably *Household Furniture* (1806). His collections were preserved into the twentieth century and are here incongruously displayed with

oriental furniture. Their sale in 1917, however, prompted a revival of interest in Hope's design. The chairs seen here are now at Buscot. The house was demolished in 1967, but its mausoleum has recently been restored.

opposite

THE PICTURE ROOM AT SIR JOHN SOANE'S Museum, a photograph of 2013 showing the interior, following its restoration by Julian Harrap Architects. The museum is actually the former house of the architect Sir John Soane, which he ceaselessly developed from 1792 until his death in 1837. Through his

drawings, the changing face of the interiors is meticulously documented. This room is presented with its reconstructed picture hang and decoration of 1837. It's a top-lit space with three clearly defined internal registers: low paneling to the level of the fireplace, the grey wall area, and a white lantern above. To the left and right sides, the paintings are presented on full-height doors, or "planes"— as Soane called them—that swing out from the walls. The right plane opens into another space beyond and beneath the gallery. This method of presentation lends drama to the experience of the room.

THIS CABINET OF CURIOSITIES BEGAN
to be assembled from the 1750s by the Cobbe
family at Newbridge House, Co. Dublin. It
comprises more than 1,600 objects including
fossils, shells, and curiosities and occupies
a small museum building. The display cases
date to about 1790 and are an important and
unusual survival. Earlier collections of this
kind, such as the geological collection of
Dr. John Woodward (now at the Sedgwick
Museum of Earth Sciences, Cambridge)
or the curiosities of the seventeenth-
century traveler Dr. John Bargrave (now at
Canterbury Cathedral), tend to be arranged
in sealable cabinets without glass. A more
recent member of the family, the interior
designer Alec Cobbe, has restored the room
with Chinese wallpaper.

above

THE GREAT DRAWING ROOM OF CLIFFE
Castle, Keighley, Yorkshire, part of a
house built by the wool merchant Henry
Butterfield and completed in 1884.
Butterfield was an ardent Francophile and
lived with his wife for a period in Paris,
where they were received into the court of
Napoleon III. His house is a homage to his
memory of the city and is filled to bursting
with French paintings and works of art. As
his son later wrote, Butterfield resolved to
fill Cliffe Castle "with every costly detail
his Parisian experience could suggest."

Some specialist workmen were even brought
from France to install fittings. The wide
door openings, originally hung with heavy
curtains, create a vista through to the dining
room and music drawing room beyond.

opposite

THE CENTRAL HALL OF HARRIS MUSEUM,
Preston, Lancashire, begun in 1882 with
the fortune left to the town by the wealthy
industrialist Edmund Robert Harris.
When the town corporation agreed to
build a new library and museum with the

money in 1881, they gave the project to a
local architect, James Hibbert (who also
happened to be mayor). The new building
was Neo-Grecian and designed internally
around a vertiginous central hall, with
a lower, middle, and upper gallery. This
space incorporates plaster casts of antique
sculpture, including fragments from the
Parthenon. At the top level is a copy of an
Assyrian frieze from the British Museum
and a series of views of Ancient Egypt by
John Somerscales, commissioned by the
town and painted in about 1909–13.

above left

IN 1893 SIR HARRY VERNEY ESTABLISHED a museum at Claydon House, Buckinghamshire, in the top-lit lobby at the head of the main staircase. It was furnished with objects collected by his son Edmund Verney in British Columbia during the 1860s. This photograph shows the collection in 1912. Particularly prominent are two house posts from a tribal village "from the mouth of the Courtenay River." Sir Harry wrote to thank his son for these objects in 1864: "If I can ever afford to build a Portico ... your beautiful carvings, like Gog and Magog, may stand on

each side to test the Courage of Visitors ... to terrify naughty children." The views of Rome to the left look prosaic by comparison. In 1931 the contents of the museum were sold.

opposite below

THE MAIN STAIRCASE AT EATON HALL, Cheshire, as photographed in 1932. It is lined with suits of armor bought from Horace Walpole's celebrated eighteenth-century collections at Strawberry Hill. The tradition of decking rooms with decorative displays of armor can be dated to the seventeenth century in England. Nevertheless, the enthusiasm for collecting and displaying armor reached a fever pitch in the nineteenth century. To furnish buyers with the necessary quantity of armor, dealers amalgamated, or pieced out, suits for visual effect. This staircase was part of the house built for the Duke of Westminster at the astonishing cost of £600,000 by Alfred Waterhouse. On its completion in 1881, the Duke wrote "now that I have built a palace, I wish I lived in a cottage." It was demolished in 1961.

above

AN ALMOST SURREALIST JUXTAPOSITION of a kissing chair and a taxidermy cockerel on a tripod in the Oak Room at Provender House, Kent. This room is paneled with salvaged material that was probably brought here from another house in the 1920s. It was furnished in eclectic taste by Constance Borgstrom, whose daughter married Prince Andrew Romanoff, eldest nephew of Tsar Nicholas II of Russia. This striking image underlines the power of curious objects, however strange they may be, to dominate a room and command interest.

previous pages

SIR LOUIS DU PAN MALLET, A FORMER British ambassador to Constantinople, purchased Wardes at Otham, Kent, in 1905. At the time, this medieval and Elizabethan house had been divided up into several cottages. With the practical assistance of his brother, he repaired the fabric and reintegrated the cottages to form a single house. Shown here is the "living room" in the Elizabethan wing with the "parlour" beyond in 1919. It is a connoisseur's interior, with fine pieces of furniture, works of art, and books carefully arranged for the benefit of the camera. The architect and interior designer Philip Tilden had a hand in the decoration of the room.

above

OUR UNDERSTANDING OF GRAND medieval residential architecture is almost entirely derived from the evidence of surviving masonry buildings. That makes Ockwells Manor, Berkshire, a unique survival from a tradition of high-quality timber-frame residential architecture about which we know little. It was probably begun in 1446 by the courtier Sir John Norreys as a hunting lodge. The hall, shown here, preserves a complete cycle of heraldic glass (windows at upper right), probably made by the king's glazier, John Prudde. The background glass comprises motto bands and diamond quarries with three distaffs bound together, a reference to Sir John's service to the queen. Brian Stein assembled the collection shown here.

opposite

THE DANCER, 1913, BY THE FRENCH sculptor Henri Gaudier-Brzeska (1891–1915) framed in sunlight at Kettle's Yard, Cambridge. The figure was cast in 1967 from a plaster original. Kettle's Yard was the open house and art gallery of Jim and Helen Ede from 1957 to 1973. They created their home here, from what had formerly been four derelict cottages, and filled it with furniture, art, and ceramics. Ede had been a curator at the Tate Gallery in London and gave tours of his house and its collection. The house was further extended with a new room suitable for concerts, designed by Professor Sir Leslie Martin and David Owers. In 1973 Kettle's Yard became the modern and contemporary art gallery of the University of Cambridge. After a recent renovation, it remains a thriving museum and gallery.

above

A FORMER BEDROOM AT SNOWSHILL
Manor, Gloucestershire, filled with samurai
armor and a Spanish shrine. Snowshill was
bought in 1919 by Charles Paget Wade after
he saw the house advertised in *Country Life*
while he was serving in the trenches. Wade
was an obsessive collector, who reveled
in the romantic association of objects.
He chose to acquire objects with strict
regard for principles of design, color, and
workmanship, and he gradually filled not
only the house, but also the garden (where
he laid out a model village). There are also
collections of instruments, weights, bicycles,
toys, and much else besides. Wade was a
friend of the architect Albert Richardson, a
notable collector of Georgian objects.

opposite

THE CABINET OF CURIOSITIES,
or *Wunderkammer* ("wonder chamber"),
assembled at Wenlock Abbey, Shropshire,
since 1983 by its present owner, the artist
Louis de Wet. With its large fireplace, it is
believed the room was used by an herbalist
who would have prepared medicine for
the monastic infirmary during the Middle
Ages, when the abbey was originally built.
This cabinet comprises a bewildering
array of curious and natural objects, from
the crocodile and shark that hang from the
ceiling to the grotesque sixteenth-century
firedog and a ring supposedly containing
a lock of Marie Antoinette's hair. It is a
collection in the tradition of the Renaissance.
De Wet points to the wunderkammer at
the Schloss Ambras, Innsbruck, formed by
Archduke Ferdinand II of Austria in the
late sixteenth century, as an important
inspiration for his own collection.

opposite

THE MORNING ROOM OF AVENUE HOUSE, Ampthill, Bedfordshire, photographed in 2013. This interior was the creation of the architect Sir Albert Richardson, a leading figure in the early twentieth-century revival of Classical architecture in Britain. Richardson bought this Georgian house (begun in 1795) in 1919 and restored it. The town of Ampthill was also protected from development through his efforts. This room survived as decorated in 1919, with brown, papered walls. Richardson was delighted to live in the house as a Georgian would have, so he did not have the room electrified or centrally heated. He filled the property with Georgian objects and art. At far left is a sedan chair that he used when he could find chairmen willing to carry it. The house and contents were sold shortly after this photograph was taken.

above

THE GREEN ROOM OF MALPLAQUET House, London, photographed in 2012 when the property was the home of Tim Knox, now director of the Royal Collection, and the landscape designer and historian Todd Longstaffe-Gowan. They bought this 1740s house in 1999 when it was in poor condition and had been threatened with redevelopment. They restored the building with great care as a setting for their collection of art, which they assembled over many years. Many of the rooms have themes or playfully suggest associations between the objects. Over the chimney-piece is a portrait of the gentleman architect and MP Thomas Prowse by Thomas Gainsborough, which is flanked by suits of gala livery made for the 2nd Earl of Ashburnham in 1829.

A DISPLAY AT THE LITERARY MUSEUM created at Glenthorne, Devon, by Sir Christopher Ondaatje. With its collection of printing presses, books, and type, this room evokes the experience of Sir Christopher as a publisher. On the walls are pictures of notable literary figures and in the window is a modern stained glass depiction of the first English publisher, William Caxton, at work. The other rooms of the museum present first editions and portraits of many British and American literary figures with a particular focus on the Bloomsbury Group, a literary circle of the early twentieth century.

THE ENTERTAINMENT ROOM AT AYNHOE Park, Northamptonshire, as photographed in 2008. Its walls are hung with contemporary photographs collected by the owner of the house, James Perkins. The five-fold Venetian mirror to the right of the doorway was specially commissioned for the room. Aynhoe was rebuilt by the architect Thomas Archer from 1707 and remodeled by Sir John Soane from 1800. The character of the decoration in this room contrasts strikingly with that in the remainder of the house. There are several recent examples of country house owners concentrating their modern art collections in one interior that otherwise lacks important historic features. Through the far doors is visible part of the large plaster-cast collection also assembled by the owner, which might be considered a more conventional country house collection.

below

BETWEEN 1825 AND 1848 EVELYN JOHN Shirley created for himself a new house on the family estate at Lough Fea, Co. Monaghan. It was designed by Thomas Rickman, an architect and antiquary who famously categorized the different phases of medieval English architecture. Rickman conceived the house in an Elizabethan, or Tudor, style. In 1872 this short passage was built to connect the main house with its adjacent chapel. The present owner of the house, Philip Evelyn Shirley, has restored the chapel passage and filled it with his collection of twentieth-century art, including pieces by Harold Cohen, Peter Kinley, and Northern Irish artist David Crone.

following pages

THE READING ROOM OF WINDMILL HILL, Buckinghamshire, part of a new archives complex designed by the architect Stephen Marshall for Lord Jacob Rothschild, 4th Baron Rothschild, and the Waddesdon Estate. The interior has walls of glass, which are articulated by a minimal structure and a screen of timber. The two triangular upright frames echo the form of the deeply coffered oak ceiling that covers the interior. It's a detail that also recurs in miniature on the legs of the reading tables and in the steel legs of the chairs. The new building is filled with art. At each end of the room is a striking work of contemporary art. The one visible here is *Untitled* by Anish Kapoor (2009).

4

Tudor & Jacobean

IN 1900, *COUNTRY LIFE* PUBLISHED *THE SHAKESPEARE COUNTRY*, its first book. Produced on the same presses that printed the magazine, it was a lyrical account of the history and antiquities of Warwickshire. Here, in the geographic heartlands of England, the book suggests, amid ancient churches, country houses, and timber-frame villages, lies the essence of England. In the back of the book was a map to help readers explore the riches it presented while driving a new invention that would revolutionize modern travel: the motorcar.

The Shakespeare Country illustrates the way in which nineteenth-century Britain went in search of its cultural soul. The place where it repeatedly discovered that soul—often with a degree of wishful thinking—was the Tudor world of the sixteenth century. This was the period when England and Scotland rejected the power of the Catholic Church in Rome and, through the Reformation, discovered their Protestantism; when English as a distinct language found its voice through the work of its most celebrated playwright; and when the institution of Parliament articulated national sovereignty for the first time.

Such elevated themes were interwoven with memorable and very colorful historical personalities. This was the world of Henry VIII and his lurid marital affairs, and of Elizabeth I enthroned as England's virgin queen. No less significant were events that occurred after the death of Elizabeth, the last Tudor, in 1603—her successor, the Stuart king James VI of Scotland, integrated the two kingdoms of England and Scotland to establish Great Britain and gave his name to its national flag, the Union Jack. He ruled England as James I and lent his name to a decorative style that took to extremes the aesthetic preferences of the Tudor style—the Jacobean.

Small surprise that in architecture and fashion, the Tudor world—and that of the Stuarts prior to the Civil War in the mid-1600s, the Jacobean—underwent a remarkable revival in the nineteenth century. It was a style at once suffused with history and distinctively British. Yet what constituted that style?

The Tudor style was essentially a refinement of the late phase of English Gothic architecture, referred to as the Perpendicular. It was characterized by a delight in regularity of detail and the overlay of surfaces with webs of geometric ornament, particularly rectilinear grids. These might be created using the timbers of a structural frame or paneling. Wherever possible such grids were opened up to create massive windows. In the most sophisticated buildings external walls might be angled or bowed outward to create multifaceted "compass windows." The name is a reference to the mason's tool—the compass—necessary to lay out their complex geometry.

The interest in grids, or webs, of geometric ornament extended to the treatment of ceilings. In domestic apartments these were often molded from white plaster to reflect light into the room. Their surfaces were also decorated with complex lattices of ribs and pendants derived from Gothic vault design. Some also borrow from the English tradition of paneled timber roofs, as is the case with the earliest known example of a domestic plaster ceiling at Great Chalfield, Wiltshire, dating to the 1460s. In both architecture and furnishing, the Tudor and Jacobean styles delighted in applied decoration. This was viewed as a mark of opulence, so for most patrons, the more ornament you could fit onto ceilings, fireplaces, furniture, and architecture, the better.

The revival of the Tudor and Jacobean styles in the nineteenth century also brought about the revival of an associated tradition of construction. During the course of the preceding century, the practice of building timber-frame houses had almost completely disappeared, partly because of the associated risk of fire. Now it resurged as a feature of revived Tudor architecture in buildings of every scale. The fascination persisted into the mid-twentieth century, when housing developments of Tudor-style homes sprang up, along with "olde-worlde" pubs, and even—dangerously—petrol stations with thatched pumps.

Concurrent with the trend to build new Tudor-style buildings was an equally important interest in preserving the real ones. Previous to the 1870s, a fashionable country house was by definition a modern one. Old seats that had not been modernized, if they survived at all, tended to end up as farm houses or even cottages. From the 1870s on, the British became increasingly interested in a completely new phenomenon: the revival of historic houses.

THE PARLOR OF ALSTON COURT, Suffolk, is a superbly preserved interior of about 1520. A characteristic feature of the period is the continuous line of high windows. This arrangement permitted fabrics to be hung over the lower register of the wall. The paneling seen here was installed in 1630, but, remarkably, a fragment of painted cloth has been discovered behind it. Cloth painted with figurative scenes—a cheap alternative to tapestry—was a common form of English domestic decoration into the seventeenth century. The timbers of the structure and paneling create dense grids of the kind favored by the aesthetic of the Perpendicular. None of the furniture is original to this room; much of that seen here is seventeenth century.

THE LONG GALLERY OF HATFIELD House, Hertfordshire. The house was built between 1607 and 1611 by Robert Cecil, Earl of Salisbury, one of the most powerful figures in the courts of Elizabeth I and James I. Both the paneling and the fireplaces, the latter painted to look like marble, were designed by the carpenter called Jenever. The gallery was extended in the 1780s, and its plaster ceiling, original to the room, was gilded in the nineteenth century.

Long-neglected medieval and Tudor properties suddenly became highly desirable and were pressed back into use by the wealthy. Such revival was often associated with radical modernization, but during this period, it was combined with great pride in their history and a desire to preserve the character that grew out of that heritage. In the process, the mid-Victorian great house, in which every household and social function was carried out in a specially designated room, necessarily gave way.

While a historic building could be added on to and expanded with new service buildings, ancient houses rarely possessed large numbers of domestic rooms. To make the most of those that existed, therefore, these spaces had to be used flexibly. By 1900, such informality aligned with the changing social use of country houses. The rapidly growing popularity of the motorcar made days-long formal house parties a thing of the past, since the smart set could now simply drop by for lunch.

The revival of old buildings and the appreciation of their historic fabric was intimately bound up with—and informed—the Arts and Crafts movement, a connection that's still very much in evidence in twenty-first century essays in the Tudor style.

opposite

THE LONG GALLERY OF LITTLE MORETON
Hall, Cheshire, built in about 1560. Its
timber frame structure picturesquely twists
and turns out of the perpendicular, and the
windows cast sunlight across the elm boards
of the floor. Long, straight, open galleries like
this were used in the sixteenth century for
relaxation and recreation in poor weather.
They were sometimes hung with portraits.
Every surface is ornamented with regular
patterns: the walls and windows by grids
of paneling and timber, and the roof with
cusped wheels. The roof structure has had
to be strengthened over time, obscuring an
image of Knowledge holding the Sphere
of Destiny at the far end of the room. The
figure was copied from the title page of a
book, evidence of the use of printed sources
for inspiration.

above

THE GREAT CHAMBER OF LOSELEY PARK,
Surrey, was built in the 1560s and has as
its focal point a fireplace that rises the full
height of the room. The ceiling is decorated
with plaster ribs and pendants that project
into the room. Its white surface reflects
the light and brightens the interior. Every
fitting is encrusted with ornament, to the
Elizabethan eye a clear mark of splendor.
The central upright of the window to the
far right is carved in the form of a lion's paw
(not visible). This detail is almost certainly
borrowed from an illustration in a book
about architecture, likely imported. In its
original form, this room would probably
have been sparsely furnished and laid with
woven matting rather than carpets, a highly
prized covering more commonly laid over
tables than on the floor.

above

THE GREAT CHAMBER, OR GREAT DINING room, at Knole, Kent, created by the 1st Earl of Dorset in about 1608. Its fireplace, a virtuoso work of white, grey, and black marble, was almost certainly carved by Cornelius Cure, the king's master mason. Cure was of Dutch descent but English born and based in Southwark, a suburb of London, which was a center of tomb manufacturing, an industry that specialized in marble carving. Both the paneling and the rich carved decoration of the internal cornice were probably also executed by London craftsmen. The joinery incorporates motifs copied from pattern books published in Italy and the Netherlands. The elaborate velvet and gold furnishings are late additions to the room. They stand out brilliantly against its pale palette.

opposite

THE HALL OF MIDDLE TEMPLE, LONDON, completed in 1570, is still used today as a dining chamber by barristers who eat in groups, or messes, of four; it is forbidden to converse between messes. With its great open roof, the hall is essentially medieval in form. Against the far wall is the screen that separates the hall from the kitchen and other services. It was in this space that Shakespeare's play *Twelfth Night* was first performed in 1602. The screen would have been the backdrop, with the two doors serving as stage entrance and exit. The first purpose-built theaters in London were similarly designed with a backdrop containing two doors beneath a balcony, an arrangement borrowed directly from the conventional design of hall screens like this.

following pages

THE GREAT CHAMBER OF GILLING CASTLE, Yorkshire, was created in about 1575. Most of the internal fittings in the room, including the paneling and stained glass, were bought by William Randolph Hearst shortly before World War II and miraculously survived the conflict while sitting in packing cases on Liverpool docks. The decorative theme of the interior is heraldry. Along the cornice circling the entire room are the shields of every gentry family in Yorkshire hung on trees representing the "hundreds," or administrative districts, in which they lived. The ancestors of the families associated with the castle are depicted in the stained-glass windows. Unusually, the designer of the interior, Baernard Dininckhoff, a German based in York, left his signature in the stained glass.

opposite

THE GREAT HALL OF WOLLATON, Nottinghamshire, completed in 1588 and designed by the mason and surveyor Robert Smythson. The hall, which rises through the center of the building, is lit on four sides by traceried windows and covered in a massive open timber roof. Pendants and coats of arms decorate the roof, which springs from bosses that are carved as grimacing satyrs' heads. The screen that by convention closes off the kitchen and other services is constructed of stone and ornamented with strapwork, a type of decoration composed of thick curving borders. Above the screen is a seventeenth-century organ, a reminder that halls were also used for entertainment of all kinds.

above

ONE END OF THE LONG GALLERY AT Haddon Hall, Derbyshire, completed in about 1580. The outward walls of the room are pierced by massive grid windows that preserve large amounts of sixteenth-century glass set in diamond-shaped quarries leaded together. These let in the light but are difficult to see through. Cut into the glass are many inscriptions and verses left over the centuries by visitors. The wall paneling is architectural in form and, as is conventional for this period, incorporates three horizontal registers, a lower dado, a middle band, and a cornice, just below the ceiling, decorated with heraldry. On the apex of the door to the left is the figure of a peacock, the crest of the Manners family, Earls and Dukes of Rutland.

left

THE USE OF POLISHED STONE OR MARBLE in many colors was particularly admired in the Tudor period and was understood to suggest Roman decoration. In the Best Bedchamber (now the Green Velvet Room) of Hardwick Hall, Derbyshire, there is an unusually opulent 1590s scheme of alabaster and blackstone paneling that extends across a fireplace, a door, and the adjacent walls. It was probably carved by the very highly paid craftsman Thomas Accres. The finish is in striking contrast to the wooden paneling of the remainder of the room and also of the tapestry just visible inside the chamber beyond, the most prized of all wall coverings during this period. Decorative marble work of this kind was vastly expensive. It was used in tomb monuments and imitated in wall painting schemes.

above

THE ORIEL WINDOW OF THE GREAT chamber at Stockton House, Wiltshire, was built in about 1610 by the wealthy London clothier John Topp. Oriels, or projecting windows, were spaces set apart, forming a room within a room into which the owner or privileged guests could retire for more intimate conversation or to take in the view. They were a common feature in both halls and great chambers from the late fourteenth century onward. Here the importance of the space is emphasized by the large pendant vault of plaster, which is ornamented with human faces. The ring at the bottom of the pendant might have supported a candelabrum.

THE GREAT CHAMBER AT BROUGHTON
Castle, Oxfordshire, can be dated to 1599
from an inscription in the plasterwork
ceiling. Its richly carved paneling is divided
up into sections by timber pilasters that rise
the full height of the walls. In the left corner
of the room is an internal porch—literally
a projecting case for the door—to keep out
drafts. It was possibly moved here from
another room in the castle. The porch is
a prominent decorative feature with tall
obelisks and the family coat of arms over it.
The fireplace to the left was reconfigured in
the seventeenth century and the furniture is
not original to the room. The plaster ceiling
was so admired in the nineteenth century
that the Victoria and Albert Museum made
plaster molds of it, and now Victorian and
Edwardian copies of it appear in houses
across the country.

THE SO-CALLED STAR CHAMBER OF THE Little Castle at Bolsover, Derbyshire, which was created about 1630. The chamber takes its name from the plaster ceiling (recently restored), which is studded with gilded stars. The painted wooden wall paneling comprises three horizontal registers, each decorated to different effect. The dado below the windows is grained to imitate timber, and the area above this, facing into the room, is painted with Old Testament figures. By contrast, the middle surfaces flanking the windows display pairs of saints in shades of gray or grisaille. In the upper register, or cornice, are coats of arms surrounded by strapwork decoration. The fireplace made up of various polished marbles is the focus of the room.

opposite

BETWEEN 1630 AND 1631, SIR JOHN Kederminster built a screen pew for his family in the parish church of Langley Marish, Berkshire. Directly attached to the pew is this library, which contains his collection of books, mainly patristic writings. The books are stored in painted cupboards around the walls. In the fireplace is a display of heraldry with the central arms of Sir John chained in a web to those of other related families. Tiny hands grasp the ends of these connecting chains. In the angles of the overmantle are images of the virtues. The whole room and its contents may simply be Sir John's study, which was brought to the church from his nearby home following his death.

above

ASTON HALL ON THE OUTSKIRTS OF Birmingham was probably designed by the London-based surveyor John Thorpe and was completed in 1635. The house was badly damaged during the Civil War a decade or so later, and in the late eighteenth century, the entrance hall, shown here, was redecorated in a consciously Jacobean style with a decorative plaster ceiling, a cornice of animals, paneling, and strapwork decoration over the door. The inscription above the fireplace, probably from this later Georgian period, exhorts servants to remain "silent faithfull just and true, content to take some paine." The Georgian interest in Jacobean architecture has never been properly explored and well-executed recreations are easy to look through.

above

IN 1822 GREGORY GREGORY, THE
eccentric owner of Harlaxton Manor,
determined to build himself a Jacobean
mansion. According to his own account,
because there were "few or no books on
the subject, he examined personally most
of the houses in Britain in that style." He
claimed to have visited at least 19 buildings,
including Bramshill, Hardwick, Longleat,
and Temple Newsam, as well as many
smaller properties and university buildings.
Work to the new house began in the 1830s
and the hall, shown here, is representative
of its extraordinarily bold conception. It was
designed by the architect Anthony Salvin.
The ceiling is supposedly modeled on that of
Audley End, Essex.

opposite

THE DINING ROOM AT THIRLESTANE
Castle, Berwickshire, in Scotland was
constructed in the 1840s by the Edinburgh
architects William Burn and David Bryce.
The core of the present castle was the
creation of the Duke of Lauderdale in the
late seventeenth century. This room was
one of several nineteenth-century additions
intended to adapt the building to Victorian
standards. The interior is made Jacobean
by its pendant, plaster ceiling. Burn came
to specialize in this style, perhaps because
one of his first English projects was the
completion of Harlaxton Manor from 1838.
The walls are hung with family portraits.

left

THE MASTER'S LODGE OF ST. JOHN'S College, Cambridge, was rebuilt by Sir George Gilbert Scott between 1863 and 1865. Externally, the building is Gothic in style but the interior preserves some remarkable Tudor elements. Shown here is a view of the Oak Room, which incorporates a ceiling and paneling (as well as a window) preserved from the original master's lodge that was destroyed by Scott's wider alterations to the college. In effect, this chamber is the recreated room of the founding master of the college, John Fisher, Bishop of Rochester, whose portrait hangs above the fireplace. The recycling of original materials for this interior was probably overseen by Scott's son. His respectful approach reflects the massive change that overtook the treatment of historic buildings in the 1870s and beyond.

below left

THIS MEDIEVAL TIMBER FRAME ROOM originally came from Carr Street in Ipswich. It now forms part of Ashby St. Ledgers Manor, Northamptonshire, a house adapted and enlarged by the architect Edwin Lutyens from 1907 for the Hon. Ivor Guest and his new wife, the Hon. Alice Grosvenor. In 1908 this Ipswich house was exhibited at the Franco-British exhibition at White City, which got is name from the fact that the buildings constructed for the event were painted white. The interiors are an Edwardian confection with plaster panels in a Renaissance style, Gothic radiator grills, and tinted glass. They perfectly express the late-Victorian taste for Tudor architecture, but it's a mark of editorial disapproval that *Country Life* did not photograph this interior when it first featured the house in 1951.

opposite

BETWEEN 1899 AND 1901, THE FOUNDER of *Country Life*, Edward Hudson, commissioned the architect Edwin Lutyens to create a new home, the Deanery, Berkshire. This photograph of the hall was taken soon after the completion of the building. It shows an Arts and Crafts realization of a late medieval English hall with an open-timber roof and oriel window. The timber framing defines every element of the design, and at the right the wall is filled in with blocks of white chalk in striking contrast to the dark timber patterns. Filling the interior are numerous pieces of seventeenth-century furniture, which Hudson avidly collected. It was much in fashion at the time.

opposite

IN THE 1920s THE LAST EARL OF
Berkeley engaged in the extravagant
remodeling of his castle at Berkeley,
Gloucestershire, which remains the
seat of the family today. The earl was
a cosmopolitan figure who divided his
time between Italy and California, but in
his castle—with the help of the London
decorating firm of Herbert Keeble—he
worked in a considered antiquarian style.
Materials and fittings were bought in
Europe to furnish the building. Shown
here is a huge Jacobean bed in the master
bedroom. On the wall are stamped leather
hangings, and the door to the right leads
to his dressing room. The ceiling lamp
and other light fixtures were designed to
suit the interior, and were electrified by
the earl.

above left

A PHOTOGRAPH OF 1919 SHOWING
the great hall of Beaudesert, Staffordshire.
Between 1909 and 1912, and following
a fire, the owner of the house, Captain
Harry Lindsey, oversaw the complete
renovation of the building. In the process,
all evidence of a nineteenth-century
Gothic remodeling were stripped away.
Lindsey was the uncle of the Duke
of Rutland and involved in the 1920s
restoration of Haddon Hall in Derbyshire.
The hall, shown here, was reconstructed
to emulate the house as it might have
appeared when it was owned by the
bishops of Coventry and Lichfield in the
Middle Ages. Captain Lindsey bought
the tapestries and massive oak table to
furnish the interior in what he imagined
was authentic Tudor style. The property
was sold and demolished in 1935.

left

HIGH GLANAU MANOR, MONMOUTH-
shire, was the home of Henry Avray
Tipping, architectural editor of *Country
Life* from 1907 to 1933. He worked on
the house and gardens in 1922–23, the
former in collaboration with Eric Francis.
Tipping was an important influence on
the early development of the magazine
and his tastes were reflected in its pages.
The so-called Living Room, shown here
in a photograph of 1929, lies at the center
of the house. With its plasterwork ceiling,
the room could be Tudor or Jacobean. The
single place setting at the seventeenth-
century table—just one of numerous
beautiful furnishings in the room—is
powerfully suggestive of a collector's
refined but isolated life.

IN 1922 PARHAM HOUSE, WEST SUSSEX, was bought by Viscount Cowdray for his son and daughter-in-law, Clive and Alysia Pearson. They found the Elizabethan building, begun in 1577 by one Thomas Palmer, neglected and denuded of its furnishings. The Pearsons set to work recreating the house both as a home and a museum collection. They stripped back and repaired the fabric with exemplary care and then purchased furniture, fabrics, and art to fill it. Shown here is the long gallery, which is filled with some of the objects they amassed. The ceiling painting was executed by the stage designer Oliver Messel in 1967–68.

RYCOTE HOUSE, OXFORDSHIRE, WAS rebuilt on a grand scale during the reign of Queen Mary I (or Mary Tudor) in the sixteenth century and then demolished in 1807. Only one section of this important building survived, and since 2000 it has been restored and enlarged as a private residence by Mr. and Mrs. Bernard Taylor. One new addition to the building is this double-height dining room, which has been designed in a Jacobean style by Nicholas Thomson of Donald Insall Associates. Its barrel-vaulted strapwork ceiling in fibrous plaster was created by Hayles and Howe of Bristol, and the stone chimneypiece was built by master mason Mark Devlin and carved by the Filkins Stone Company. The silver sconces were made by Dernier and Hamlyn.

THE LONG GALLERY OF CROSBY HALL, London, is a newly created Tudor interior that enjoys spectacular views across the River Thames. Since his purchase of the property in 1988, Dr. Christopher Moran has developed Crosby Hall as a setting for his collection of Tudor art and furnishings. His aim has been to "bring together the art and architecture of the Tudor period, increasing their meaning by displaying them in an appropriate context."

right

THIS DINING ROOM WAS CREATED IN about 1611 as part of alterations to South Wraxall Manor, Wiltshire. It originally served as a parlor, a room for informal gatherings and conversation. The massive fireplace is original to the room and one of several unusually opulent examples in the house. It is carved with aphorisms in Latin. Such texts on a religious or moral theme were a popular feature of Tudor and Stuart domestic interiors particularly in Protestant households. The parlour was converted into a dining room around 1700, when it was repaneled and provided with a recess for the display of ceramics (part of which is just visible to the right). Since their purchase of the property in 2005, the current owners, John Taylor of the band Duran Duran and Gela Nash-Taylor, co-founder of Juicy Couture, have restored the house. Among those involved in the project has been the interior decorator Robert Kime.

following pages

THE KING JAMES DRAWING ROOM AT Hatfield House, Hertfordshire, is an early seventeenth-century interior. It takes its name from the image of the monarch that presides above the fireplace. The room was refurnished in the late eighteenth century and redecorated several times in the nineteenth and twentieth centuries. During these changes, the walls were hung with full-length portraits creating an interior that was grand but not particularly warm. On the advice of Alec Cobbe, the present Lord Salisbury has hung the walls with seventeenth-century tapestry, creating a sumptuous background to a collection of Flemish and Italian paintings. The overlay of tapestry and paintings in this way is brilliantly successful but would have seemed strange in the seventeenth century, as the imagery of the tapestries would have been considered more important.

THE HALL, BRADFORD ON AVON,
Wiltshire, was built about 1600 and was
described by the seventeenth-century
antiquarian John Aubrey as "The best
built house for the quality of a gentleman
in Wilts." Along with Hardwick Hall,
Derbyshire, it is perhaps the supreme
surviving illustration of the Elizabethan
desire to create buildings with walls of
glass (though the glass seen here is in fact
nineteenth century). Here the central
window incorporates a central bow or
projection. This splendid room became the
study of the late Dr. Alex Moulton and is
shown here, preserved as he knew it, in a
photograph of 2018. Among his particular
interests were vehicle suspension and
the design of folding bicycles, hence the
celebrated Moulton brand. His factory
stands immediately beneath the house.

Baroque

IN THE SPRING OF 1613, THOMAS HOWARD, EARL OF ARUNDEL, SET out from England for Germany with his wife, Countess Aletheia. They formed part of a glittering entourage conducting the king's daughter, Princess Elizabeth, to her new husband, the Elector Palatine, in Heidelberg. Having completed this duty, the Earl and Countess continued with special royal license through the Alps to Italy. It was a journey that would help change the architectural face of England and with it the grand domestic interior.

Traveling with the Earl and Countess was one Inigo Jones, a London-born joiner, who spoke Italian and was recommended to the party as a translator, as well as for his knowledge of both the region and its art. Jones had already established himself as a set designer of elaborate entertainments called masques, in which courtiers acted out allegorical scenes against theatrical backdrops dressed in splendid costumes. He also had an interest in architecture informed by technical publications on the subject, which he avidly acquired. Sometimes alone, and sometimes in the company of his noble patrons, he now examined the art, architecture, and classical ruins of northern Italy and Rome.

Early in 1615, following his return to England, Jones summarized his ideas and observations in a travel notebook. Architecture, he thought, should be "Sollid, proporsionable according to the rulles, masculine and unaffected." Internally, however, Jones thought it should be varied with "composed internal ornament." To illustrate the point, he drew an analogy between architecture and a wise man who "carrieth a graviti in Publicke Places ... y[e]t inwardly hath his Immaginacy set on fire ... to dellight, amase us sumtimes [move] us to laughter, sumtimes to contemplation and horror."

Exposure to Italian ideas through treatises was nothing new in England in 1615. The idiomatic and eclectic Neo-Classicism that Jones absorbed at first hand on his travels in Italy, however, was quite different from the architecture his English predecessors had learned in books. Through Thomas Howard's support and through his post as surveyor of the King's Works, responsible for all royal buildings, he won several prominent London building projects. Three of these would pass into the bloodstream of English architecture: the Banqueting House designed for the royal palace of Whitehall; the west front of St. Paul's Cathedral; and the Queen's House in Greenwich (not to mention his involvement in London's first public square, or piazza, Covent Garden).

Prominent though these buildings were, they were created for an exclusive court circle and seemingly exercised little influence on the mainstream of contemporary Jacobean architecture (shaped, as we have seen, by late medieval and Tudor taste). And if they were to be judged against contemporary developments in Italian architecture in the early seventeenth century, they were extremely old fashioned. Nevertheless, they had an important afterlife when Civil War in the 1640s destroyed the court and Jones's career. Though he was fortunate to walk away from the siege of Basing House, he died soon afterward in 1652.

Shortly after his death, however, the ideas that Jones had promulgated enjoyed—both directly and indirectly—great popularity among those who formed the new administration. In particular, they took to the idea of a symmetrical house with a central door, tall rectangular windows, and a high-pitched roof. Given its ubiquity today, it is difficult to imagine that in mid-seventeenth-century England it was revolutionary.

The interiors of these homes maintained a long-existing distinction between public and domestic interiors. The public areas—usually the hall and principal stair—were finished in natural stone and marble (or were colored to appear as if they were) and assumed a strictly architectural form. In proportion they were usually boxier than Tudor interiors, with deep curving surfaces called coves connecting the walls to high, flat ceilings.

By contrast, the private spaces of the house proper were often less consciously architectural in character. Usually they were finished with paneling—which could be overhung with tapestry or fabrics—and their ceilings were executed in plaster. As we shall see, these finishes assumed new decorative forms over time, but they were all long-standing treatments of English interior decoration. The visual centerpiece of such rooms remained the fireplace. It was almost invariably placed on one long wall of the room and was conceived as a miniaturized work of architecture.

previous pages
THE CENTERPIECE OF THE drawing room ceiling at Astley Hall, Lancashire, part of a decorative scheme of rich plasterwork in the house. It was probably created in the decade after 1666, following the marriage of the heiress Margaret Charnock, whose family had owned the manor since the thirteenth century, to one Richard Brooke. The room is very low, which makes this remarkable decorative plasterwork seem all the more striking. The sense of movement is typical of the Baroque. So too are the Neo-Classical motifs of cherubs, cockleshells, foliage, garlands, and flowers.

Such conservatism, however, did not preclude corresponding novelty. There was, for example, an interest pioneered by Jones and his patrons during the early seventeenth century in the display of art collections within houses. Portrait painting had been a prominent feature of Tudor interiors; so too had paintings fixed within the wall paneling. Now, paintings of Classical subjects, or genre pieces, started to appear and were hung in frames on the walls of private rooms. They were objects, moreover, of self-consciously dilettante admiration. Sculpture was also introduced to the domestic interior for the first time, commonly in rooms that opened directly to the outdoors. After the beheading of Charles I in 1649, the sale of his art collection, the greatest ever amassed by a British monarch, fed this appetite for collecting.

In 1660 Charles II and his Royalist circle were returned to power and began to build as a means of reasserting their authority. In Scotland, particularly through the work of the gentleman architect Sir William Bruce, the architectural forms promoted by Inigo Jones and his followers now found expression in houses such as Kinross and the royal palace of Holyrood. To the Scots, who were familiar with castle-like residences, such buildings were a complete novelty.

In England, however, a very different Neo-Classical taste prevailed, shaped in particular by the experience of the exiled King Charles II in the French court of Louis XIV. The result was a style of building flavored by the spectacular scale and fashions of Continental Baroque. Perhaps the most striking innovation of the Baroque were vast trompe l'oeil schemes that encouraged visitors to gaze through the real walls of a room into a fantasy world presenting the adventures of Classical deities. The sole English precedents for such illusions on a grand scale (though on masque themes rather than mythological ones) were the ceilings installed in the hall of the Queen's House, Greenwich (1630s) and the Banqueting Hall (1629–30), both by Inigo Jones. Ornamental ironwork, meanwhile, was employed on an unprecedented scale in the Baroque. Since it was possible to see through it, ironwork allowed for the visual interplay of spaces, an idea also reinforced architecturally in Baroque interiors by replacing walls with screens of columns or—in domestic apartments—aligning doors between a series of rooms to create, when all were open, splendid long vistas known as enfilades.

Following soon after the Restoration came the Great Fire of London in 1666. It was a catastrophe that helped bring to prominence a brilliant young academic, Christopher Wren. With hardly any architectural experience, he took charge of the reconstruction of more than fifty churches in the capital, as well as its cathedral, St. Paul's. For Wren, architecture was a means of realizing in physical form his belief in the transcendent truth and beauty of geometry. He worked in an assured and dignified Classical style, and his designs are enlivened—as in the dome of St. Paul's—by a strong technical understanding of structure and an awareness of Baroque architecture in Europe, where he had traveled extensively.

Also apparent in his work is a profound sympathy for much earlier English architecture. Wren restored numerous medieval churches, which made him familiar with Gothic architecture, and in his design for the west front of St. Paul's he carefully copied details from the work of Inigo Jones. Such allusions are the first evidence that the English Neo-Classical tradition was developing an awareness of its own history. As Britain grew in wealth and power, the idea that its architecture had a national character also began to develop.

In addition to his church work, Wren worked on numerous palaces, public buildings, and houses. The outstanding figure who carried forward his particular brand of British monumental Baroque architecture into the domestic sphere, however, was Nicholas Hawksmoor. Hawksmoor trained in Wren's office but he also had a long, independent career into the 1730s. Though he never appears to have traveled, he developed an understanding of architecture through a combination of practical experience and reading. On some projects he collaborated with Sir John Vanbrugh, a soldier and a playwright. Opinion remains sharply divided as to the nature of their creative partnership. Regardless, they were formative figures in the kingdom's search for its own unique form of Neo-Classicism. It was partly a judgement on their success creating a national style that the English Baroque was revived in the late nineteenth century, giving birth to what was wittily dubbed an architectural "Wrenaissance." Their work continues to inspire today.

previous pages

THE DOUBLE CUBE ROOM AT WILTON HOUSE, Wiltshire, created in 1636–40 by Inigo Jones for Philip Herbert, 4th Earl of Pembroke, Lord Chamberlain of Charles I's household. The French hydraulic engineer Isaac de Caus probably acted as executant architect. This room, which is 60 l x 30 w x 30 h feet, has been admired since the eighteenth century as a perfectly proportioned interior (though the coving intrudes deeply into this volume). Much of the wall surface is covered by painting, a treatment ultimately inspired by Italian examples. The painting by Van Dyck on the far wall is the largest seventeenth-century canvas in Britain. The room was intended as part of a royal apartment and probably resembles the interiors of Whitehall Palace as they would have looked at that time.

opposite

THE SALOON OF FORDE ABBEY, DORSET, built after 1649, possibly to the designs of Edward Carter, Surveyor of the King's Works from 1643. The ceiling is not decorated with Gothic vaulting patterns but rectangular panels defined by moulded beams, an Italian treatment pioneered in England by Inigo Jones. Note the central arms of the patron; the medieval art of heraldry remained an abiding English obsession. A set of five tapestries hang on the walls. These are from the cycle of seven Raphael Cartoons for the Sistine Chapel in Rome bought by Prince Charles (later Charles I) at Genoa in 1623. Although the tapestries perfectly suit the room in scale and date, they are, in fact, a late addition to it and were probably produced in the English tapestry factory at Mortlake in the 1670s.

above right

THE STAIRCASE HALL OF COLESHILL HOUSE, Berkshire, photographed in 1919 before the house was gutted by fire in 1952 and then demolished. It was designed by Roger Pratt, a hugely influential Restoration architect who traveled on the Continent during the Civil War. Inigo Jones may have advised on the building, which was begun after 1649. Nearly every feature of this room would have seemed unusual, from the divided staircase with its turned balusters and carved swags of foliage, to the busts set in niches on the wall. The interior was probably painted originally in off-white to resemble masonry, the conceit being that it was made from stone or marble.

right

THE SPIRAL STAIRCASE AT THORPE HALL, Northamptonshire, a house designed by the London surveyor Peter Mills and under construction in 1654. It provides access to a viewing platform on the roof, or belvedere. Roof areas in English great houses were used for recreation and relaxation from at least the fourteenth century. The stair is a display piece made entirely from wood but painted and detailed like architectural stonework. It rises from a gallery that runs through the middle of the building.

THE SHELDONIAN THEATRE, 1664–69, was built by Christopher Wren as the graduation hall of the University of Oxford. It takes the form of a Roman theater, though the interior also exhibits an awareness of contemporary architecture in France and Italy. Roman theaters were typically open to the sky but were often shaded by fabric awnings suspended over the auditorium, an arrangement suggested in the illusionistic ceiling painting of 1667–69 by Robert Streater. He also depicts the Arts and Sciences casting down Envy, Rapine, and Ignorance in a manner probably inspired by the masque designs of Inigo Jones. The interior has recently been returned to its original color scheme comprised of four colors: white, in imitation of stone; brown for cedar wood; purple for Rance, a Flemish marble; and grey.

above

THE HALL OF SYDENHAM HOUSE, DEVON,
built by Sir Edward Wise in the 1650s. Its
magnificent Neo-Classical fireplace bears
the impaled arms of the builder and his wife,
Arabella St. John. Adam and Eve recline on
the pediment, and above their heads appears
the date 1656. A fire in 2012 seriously
damaged the room and caused the fireplace
to explode into some two hundred fragments
that were painstakingly reassembled by
Sean Wheatley and restored by Alan Lamb
of Swan Farm Studios. Traces of color

permitted a reconstruction of the original
decoration. The room interior is paneled,
and a deep window recess, or oriel (far
right), is warmed by its own fireplace.

opposite

THE INTERIOR OF THE GREAT HALL OF
Astley Hall, Lancashire. The room was
probably constructed around 1600 and
then furnished in two stages. First, in about
1620, its paneling was painted with images
of celebrated rulers copied from prints. In
the second stage, after 1666, the staircase
and spectacular ceiling were added. Both
reflect the Restoration taste for riotous
decoration. The ceiling, with its life-size
cherubs throwing stones and firing arrows,
might make a visitor feel as though they have

suddenly stumbled into a riotous party. Its deep modeling aspiring to realism is typical of the period. The fireplace is a confection added in the nineteenth century, possibly containing the salvaged remains of the original seventeenth-century structure.

following pages

AFTER THE GREAT FIRE OF LONDON IN 1666, the companies that governed specialist trades in the city were among the first to restore their buildings. Tallow Chandlers Hall began to be rebuilt in 1668. The hall was probably designed by the master bricklayer Captain John Caine, with a keen awareness of what rival companies were building. When the joiner John Symes was commissioned to create the far hall screen in 1674, for example, he was instructed to copy that of Goldsmith's Hall, the wealthiest

company in the city. Tallow Chandlers hall has deep paneling and is lit by high circular windows. Its ceiling is a nineteenth-century recreation of the original, which would have been white. This interior remains the focus of the institution's life and ritual. It is shown here set up for a feast in 2016.

above

THE GILT ROOM OF TREDEGAR HOUSE, Monmouthshire, was created in the 1670s as part of the remodeling of the house, which had been undertaken by the Hurlbutt brothers, master carpenters of Warwick, on behalf of the owner, William Morgan. The paneling is arranged in three tiers and painted to resemble walnut with gilded detailing. It also bears several paintings, including a version of Titian's *The Venus of Urbino* over the door and representations of Summer and Winter to the right. Within the richly molded ceiling, Pope Urban VIII is overcoming lust and intemperance. All the paintings are probably based on engravings, which were a common source of artistic ideas in this period. The fireplace has barley-sugar wood columns painted to imitate marble, ensuring that virtually every inch of surface is encrusted with ornament.

opposite

THE WITHDRAWING ROOM AT Thirlestane Castle, Berwickshire, a room that was created in the 1670s by the regent of Restoration Scotland, the Duke of Lauderdale. His remodeling of the castle began on August 6, 1670, when he contracted the king's mason Robert Mylne to undertake the work. It was overseen by Sir William Bruce, a cousin of his lover (and later wife), the Countess of Dysart, and the apostle of Scottish Neo-Classicism. Lauderdale's letters reveal that he collected fittings from London and installed them with specialist labor. All that survives of the original interior is the ceiling by George Dunsterfield, which incorporates gilded musical instruments. Two joiners— Heinderich Meinners and John Christian Ulrich—worked on the original wainscoting of the house from 1677. The furnishings here are all nineteenth century.

A 1910 PHOTOGRAPH OF THE MAIN staircase at Cassiobury Park, Hertfordshire, a house designed by Hugh May for the 1st Earl of Essex from about 1677. It perfectly expresses the Restoration delight in intricate, fulsome, and flowing decoration. The whole structure is of wood and seems to hang in space. It was probably originally painted to resemble stone. Charles II's celebrated escape from capture in an oak tree at Boscobel turned the oak leaf into a patriotic emblem of the Restoration. They appear in the lowest register of the staircase in this image. As Comptroller of the Works

for the king, May was intimately involved in both the remodeling of Windsor Castle as well as the reconstruction of London after the Great Fire in 1666. Cassiobury Park was demolished in 1927.

opposite

THE CHAPEL OF TRINITY COLLEGE, Oxford, was described soon after its completion in 1694 by the traveler Celia Fiennes as "a Beautifull Magnificent Structure ... the whole Chappel is Wanscoated with Walnut tree and the fine sweet [smelling] wood ... like Cedar and

of a reddish Coullr." All the furnishings, including the altar, were made by specialist artisans, many of them from London. They were assembled, however, under the direction of the Oxford joiner Arthur Frogley for the enormous sum of £1,140. As befits a Protestant chapel, the central panel over the altar is not figural but an abstract work of marquetry. Around it is exquisitely detailed sculpture in pale lime wood, probably by the sculptor Grinling Gibbons. This photograph shows the altarpiece following its recent restoration by Alan Lamb of Swan Farm Studios, Northamptonshire.

THE HEAVEN ROOM AT BURGHLEY HOUSE
is the opening chamber of a state
apartment—a sequence of withdrawing
rooms culminating with a bed chamber,
dressing room, and closet—begun by John
Cecil, the 5th Earl of Exeter in 1680 but
never finished. Here, in a space surrounded
by Classical architecture, the visitor
stumbles across the life-size scene of Mars
caught in that act of adultery with Venus
by her husband, Vulcan. It was painted by
the Neapolitan-born Antonio Verrio, who
from 1675 created the most ambitious
scheme of Baroque painted decoration in
Britain at Windsor Castle for Charles II. The
alterations to Burghley were linked to the
transformation of Chatsworth at this time,
the earl having married into the Devonshire
family, and involved many of the same
designers, artisans, and craftsmen.

above

THE DINING ROOM AT CHEVENING, KENT,
which was probably completed shortly
before it was described by the architect
Roger North in 1698. The interior is
paneled or wainscoted. As is typical of the
most elaborate paneling of the period, it
is decorated using architectural forms. It
comprises three horizontal registers: a dado
at the base, a blind arch above, and a cornice
in the form of an entablature just below
the ceiling. Dividing the wall vertically,
and articulating each section and feature
of the room, are pilasters that rise to the
cornice. Both the door and the fireplace are
surmounted by pediments, the latter on a
small scale. The furnishings visible here are
nineteenth-century additions.

opposite

THE HALL OF BOUGHTON HOUSE IS
a medieval interior remodeled in 1695 in
preparation for a visit by King William III.
Preserving this ancient interior might have
been an act of economy but it could equally
have been intended to signal the antiquity of
the house. Whatever the case, the medieval
open-timber ceiling of the room was covered
over and decorated by Louis Chéron, a rival
of the painter Antonio Verrio. Shown here
is *The Apotheosis of Hercules*, modeled on
Charles Le Brun's ceiling of the Galerie
d'Apollon in the Louvre. Also prominent is
the heraldic achievement of Ralph, 1st Duke
of Montagu, the individual who renovated the
house in the seventeeth century. The walls
are wainscoted and hung with tapestries, part
of an exceptionally rich seventeenth-century
collection still preserved here.

below

THE STATE BEDCHAMBER AT COOMBE Abbey, Warwickshire, photographed by *Country Life* in 1909. This extraordinary bed from around 1700 bears the arms, initials, and baronial crowns of the man for whom it was made, William Craven. It is executed in the manner of the émigré French upholsterer Francis Lapierre. The tall proportions are typical of the Baroque, as is the spectacular and curvaceous ornamentation of the headboard and tester. Beds were the single most expensive articles of furniture in English interiors until the nineteenth century and were the focus of

elaborate rituals borrowed from French court protocol in this period. Just visible in the top of the photograph is a rich plaster ceiling, its original monochrome white paint enlivened with color. The contents of the house were broken up in 1923.

opposite

CASTLE HOWARD, YORKSHIRE, WAS designed by John Vanbrugh and begun in 1700. The central hall is a complex but brilliant self-contained work of architecture. Viewed in cross-section from the front, it takes the form of a triumphal arch

comprising a central arch flanked by two subsidiary arches. The latter contain stairs. As the visitor experiences the room, however, the stair chambers amplify the volume of the main space. This is lent monumentality by both its huge columns and a dome (not visible here), the first large-scale structure of its kind in English domestic architecture. The hall is ornamented with sculpture. To either side of the interior are an elaborate fireplace and a niche covered in imitation marble, or scagliola. The wall and dome paintings were executed by Scott Medd in the 1960s after the originals were damaged by fire in 1940.

left

THE MAIN STAIRCASE OF EASTON
Neston, Northamptonshire, completed in
1702, is finished in a combination of natural
stone and painted surfaces that imitate
stone. From a distance, the plaster ceiling
might easily be mistaken for marble. The
niches in the walls were originally filled
with figures from the celebrated Arundel
collection of Classical sculpture and
the panels between them are painted to
resemble reliefs by Sir James Thornhill.
In typical Baroque form, the stair has a
flowing rail of gilded ironwork, which
is much less visually intrusive than the
stone or timber balustrades of the earlier
seventeenth century. It's possible that the
house was Nicholas Hawksmoor's first
major commission, but both Wren and
William Talman, a former student of Wren's,
have been credited with contributing to the
design. Major buildings of the period were
often collaborative ventures.

opposite

THE CEILING OF THE GREAT HALL
at Blenheim Palace, Oxfordshire, was
decorated in 1716 by the painter Sir
James Thornhill. It depicts the Duke of
Marlborough in Roman attire presenting
Britannia with his plan for the battle of
Blindheim in Bavaria in 1704, his decisive
victory over the Franco-Bavarian alliance
in the War of the Spanish Succession. Work
began on Blenheim Palace, or Castle, which
was named after this battle, in 1705 as an
acknowledgment of the nation's debt to the
Duke for winning the battle. John Vanbrugh,
who designed the building, has here created
a seeming impossibility of a kind beloved
by the Baroque: a ceiling floating on sixteen
glass windows. The whole palace cost the
stupendous sum of £300,000, six times the
amount of Castle Howard.

THE DINING ROOM OF ASHBY ST.
Ledgers, Northamptonshire, was added
by Edwin Lutyens in 1924. It's an interior
characteristic of his "Wrenaissance" style,
which was inspired by Wren's seventeenth-
century English Neo-Classicism. The room
is proportioned as a cube, with a deeply
coved ceiling. Its wood-paneled walls are
punctuated by tall pilasters and the whole is
dominated by a marble fireplace carved with
heavy swags of flowers, fruit, and foliage in
the manner of the celebrated seventeenth-
century wood carver Grinling Gibbons. As
originally completed, the fireplace was hung
with a painting that extended the full width

of the overmantel. In a concession to the
Tudor exterior of the building, the windows
are designed with stone grids.

above

THE INNER HALL OF SHILSTONE, DEVON,
part of a new house designed by Kit Rae-
Scott and built for Lucy and Sebastian
Fenwick in 2000. This interior is conceived
in the spirit of the 1680s, with the walls
covered in wainscot with two levels
of paneling: a dado, defining the lower
furnished level of the room, and taller panels
above that visually accentuate its height.
In a modern touch, the paneling has been
painted in strong colors that set off the pale
furnishings. The fireplace is of polished
stone and without the typical seventeenth-
century aggrandising overmantel. Its
molding—termed a bolection—resembles

the smaller but more intricate moldings
that frame the sections of paneling. This
consonance of forms helps integrate the
fireplace visually within the room.

following pages

THORNHILL, DORSET, WAS THE FAMILY
home of the English painter Sir James
Thornhill in the late seventeenth and
early eighteenth centuries. In a round of
changes, completed in 2009, this much-
adapted house was given this new top-lit
stair by its then owner, Tommy Kyle. It
was decorated with a scheme of hand-
modeled plasterwork by Geoffrey Preston,

who worked on the restoration of Uppark,
West Sussex, following a fire in 1989. The
trophies imitate the stuccowork by Giovanni
Bagutti and Giuseppe Artari at Moor Park,
Hertfordshire, which Thornhill rebuilt and
decorated in 1720–28. The detailing of the
stair, made by Clapham Joinery, and the
depth of the three-dimensional modeling of
the plasterwork imbues this interior with a
1690s character.

The Cottage

TODAY THE COTTAGE REPRESENTS ONE OF THE IDEALS OF ENGLISH country life, a manner of comfortable living on a modest scale, one without affectation or formality. It was not always so. The term *cottage*, a word derived from medieval Latin and adopted in English in the fourteenth century, was originally applied to the rough dwellings of farmers and laborers that had few amenities. These buildings were quite small and compact and were built using cheap, local materials, including timber frame, cob, rubble, and thatch.

While landowners throughout Europe have constructed such buildings to accommodate the workers on their estates since the Middle Ages, the more prosperous laborers built their own cottages. Recent surveys of England's Midland counties have revealed thousands of surviving structures that would today be described as cottages, some of them dating as far back as the thirteenth century.

Beginning in the eighteenth century, the very rich began to imagine and build cottages for themselves that were to be used primarily for recreation. These buildings assumed the architectural qualities of rural simplicity for aesthetic effect. The exterior might have been constructed in a manner almost indistinguishable from that of a laborer's cottage, but they were usually larger and made use of rustic materials—such as thatch and timber—in an exaggerated manner. Inside, they accommodated every luxury that money could buy.

The vast chasm that existed between the cottages of the poor and the wealthy is famously satirized by Jane Austen in her novel *Sense and Sensibility* (1811). Its heroine, Elinor Dashwood, has been forced by the death of her father and reduced circumstances to move with her mother and sisters from their bright, spacious country house to a small, remote cottage in Devon offered to them by a kindly cousin who took pity on them. While living there, she meets a vain, foolish young man, Robert Ferrars, who volubly congratulates her on her situation:

> *"I am excessively fond of a cottage; there is always so much comfort, so much elegance about them. And I protest, if I had any money to spare, I should buy a little land and build one myself, within a short distance of London ... I was last month at my friend Elliott's, near Dartford. Lady Elliott wished to give a dance. 'But how can it be done?' said she ... ' My dear Lady Elliott, do not be uneasy. The dining parlour will admit eighteen couple with ease; card-tables may be placed in the drawing-room; the library may be open for tea and ... and let the supper be set out in the saloon.' So if people do but know how to set about it, every comfort may be as well enjoyed in a cottage as in the most spacious dwelling." Elinor agreed to it all, for she did not think he deserved the compliment of rational opposition.*

Wildly different as they might be, the cottages of the rich and poor have always had—and continue to have—certain characteristics in common. They are built on a relatively small scale with informally arranged rooms, which are capable of being used for a variety of purposes. To the wealthy, such as Lady Elliott, who was familiar with large houses, it really might have come as a surprise that you could have a dance without a ballroom and use the library, saloon, and drawing room of her exceptionally spacious cottage in any other way than for the functions that their names implied. Certainly, it implied an informality.

Cottages have always been closely associated with their gardens, usually a small plot of land in which flowers are propagated alongside vegetables. For the rich, at least, this arrangement softens the distinction between gardening as a task necessary for survival and one of mere recreation. The garden, moreover, is the visual horizon of most cottages, but those of the very rich are sometimes designed to look further. When they do so it is from spaces that are rather too grand to be truly cottage-like, such as terraces or conservatories.

As domestic life over the last one hundred years has grown steadily more informal and servants have largely disappeared, "cottage life" in the twenty-first century has come to revolve around the kitchen. By virtue of the stove, this is typically the warmest room in the house and often doubles both as a space for dining and relaxation. The kitchen, moreover, is often the room where life in and out of doors overlaps. Its hard-wearing central table is as likely to be used for making a coq au vin or cake as it is for arranging flowers gathered from the garden. Between meals, it's likely to be the temporary repository of homely clutter, another familiar feature of modern cottage life.

previous pages

THE GARDEN ROOM AT COMPTON END, Hampshire, was built around 1910 as part of alterations that were carried out on an ancient farmhouse. The large windows, overlooking a small garden, were made with old shop fronts bought in the local town of Winchester (as was, probably, the antique furniture). The windows created a sun-trap that, according to an article published in *Country Life* in 1919, "can be used for meals with the doors open and without a fire on a bright winter's day." To increase the light levels in the room, the whole interior is painted white. The floor tiles connect the interior to the walks in the garden beyond.

above

THE GROUND-FLOOR ROOM OF a fifteenth-century timber-frame cottage now incorporated within a much larger house known as Alston Court, Suffolk. The room has a low ceiling, an indication of its relatively modest status, and the beams are carved with decorative moldings. There are leaded windows, and the furniture is arranged around a brick chimney stack that projects into the volume of the room. Suspended from a beam to the right of the fireplace is a blue glass globe, or witches ball. Witches, it was thought, did not like to see their own reflections, so balls like this were hung to keep them away. This is a modern version of a ball shown in an early twentieth-century photograph of the room.

following pages

THE "ARCHITECT'S CORNER" OF Snowshill Manor, Gloucestershire, in 1927, an Edwardian vision of a cottage interior with simple furniture and a huge hearth. It was the creation of the architect and antiquarian Charles Wade, who transformed a former dairy wing attached to this rambling house into his lodging. Wade rescued the neglected property in 1919 at a time that the Cotswolds was enjoying enormous popularity among the wealthy in search of history. Much of the house was given over to his insatiable appetite for collecting. *Country Life* lavished praise on the result: "no mere gallery, neither is it a museum, yet a more unique collection of minor objects of national interest would be difficult to name."

THE PARLOR OF ASLACKBY MANOR,
Lincolnshire, a modest seventeenth-
century house that was sympathetically
restored by its owner, Alan Baxter, before
this photograph was taken in 2012. With
its low-ceiling rooms, many of the interiors
possess the intimacy of a spacious cottage.
The only feature in this room that suggests
a slightly grander reality are the stained
glass panels of heraldry in the windows.
All the paneling has been re-grained, a
painted finish that gives the illusion of an
even, veneered surface. The careful choice
of furniture bestows on this serene interior
the character of a seventeenth-century
Dutch painting.

ENDSLEIGH COTTAGE, DEVON, OCCUPIES
a spectacular position on the River Tamar
and was built in 1810 for the Duke and
Duchess of Bedford. The site of the cottage
was personally chosen by the duchess,
and the building itself was designed by Sir
Jeffry Wyatville. Endsleigh was a romantic
retreat for the Bedfords and was conceived
in contrast to the family's grand principal
seat at Woburn. In place of columns, the
eaves are supported by rugged timbers. The
floor is laid with actual sheep's bones. Such
buildings are today commonly described
as cottage *ornées*, or ornamental cottages,
buildings that assume the appearance of
rustic simplicity for decorative effect.

above

THE KITCHEN OF STONEYWELL COTTAGE, Leicestershire, a holiday home built in the 1890s by a proponent of the Arts and Crafts movement, Ernest Gimson, for his brother and sister-in-law. For Gimson, the word *cottage* implied a structure made by a craftsman (rather than designed by an architect), and the whole aspires to a simplicity of decoration and furnishing. The great stones in the walls were constructed from materials found on site, and the far steps are cut out of the living rock. Though a fire in 1939 seriously damaged the building, it was bought by the National Trust and returned to its mid-twentieth-century appearance.

opposite

WERN ISAF, CONWY, WAS BUILT BY the little-known Arts and Crafts architect Herbert L. North in 1900 as part of a small sea-side development at Llanfairfechan in Wales. It was his family home and designed on an unusual V-shape plan. The drawing room of the cottage, shown here, is one of three small interiors overlooking the garden. These rooms are divided by glass doors, which help keep the interior well lit and allow it to be opened out for entertainment. The William Morris curtain can also be drawn over the door to keep out drafts. North made some of the simple, robust furniture in the house.

following pages

BABYLON, OR THE WHITE HOUSE, is a 1930s holiday cottage on the shore of Lambay Island, Co. Dublin. The kitchen is extremely simple, almost Spartan, with its bare brick walls, a woven rush floor, a plain white ceiling, and wooden furniture. Against these natural tones, the blue curtains and crockery are particularly striking. The impression is of a room perfectly suited to the practical needs of holiday life: there is plenty of space to shrug off coats and shoes when a voraciously hungry family arrives back from a day-long foray outdoors.

opposite

THE CELEBRATED COTSWOLD FURNITURE
designer Gordon Russell created these
cedar cabinets for the display of a glass
collection in the study at Tower Close in
Gloucestershire in about 1920. He made
them for his father, who bought up and
restored this property—a farmhouse
that had been neglected and divided into
three cottages—in 1916. The cabinets are
exquisitely finished and conceal radiators
at the bottom, a modern comfort that would
otherwise intrude awkwardly into this
rambling interior with its natural finishes of
stone, timber, and plaster.

above

IN THE 1930s A CORNISH ARTIST,
Newton Penprase, began work on Bendhu,
a modernist house on the spectacular Antrim
coast. Penprase—or "Pen" as he was known—
taught in the Belfast School of Art for more
than forty years and continued working on
the house throughout his life. It was never
completely finished internally, though the
structure was substantially complete by
1949. Shown here is the drawing room and its
modern stove. Over the fireplace is the outline
of a semicircular table that can be folded
down from the wall to stand clear of the
hearth; it looks like a mantelpiece. The house
is full of ingenious fittings made by Pen. The
interior has recently been sympathetically
restored by its present owners.

IN 1995 THE ARCHITECT CRAIG HAMILTON and his wife, artist Diana Hulton, bought Coed Mawr in Radnorshire. The earliest parts of the house belong to a farm that was probably built here around 1500. Hamilton has greatly expanded the building in his own distinctive Neo-Classical style. The old library, however, preserves something of the character of the modest centuries-old building they inherited, with its low timber ceiling and small windows. The furniture was designed by Craig Hamilton and is architectural in character; the table and the angles of the bookshelves are supported by columns.

THE BREAKFAST ROOM AT RED HOUSE outside Aldeburgh, Suffolk. The Red House was home to the composer Benjamin Britten and his partner, the singer Peter Pears. They moved into this modest farm in 1957 and furnished it with a combination of old and new pieces, some of which came from Sweden and Italy. Pears particularly liked the combination of red and green, which is seen here in the carpet and the garden beyond. The room is hung with pictures of local views. Breakfast rooms in cottages are usually bright and open directly out to a garden.

above

THE KITCHEN OF PREHEN HOUSE, DERRY.
Although it serves a large house, this room
has the simple and functional aesthetic of a
cottage kitchen. The flagstone floor is hard
wearing and the main pieces of furniture are
painted so that they won't easily stain. By
contrast, the table surface has been left as
natural wood so that it can be easily cleaned
and won't show marks. Despite the relative
darkness of the room, it is brightened
significantly by its white walls. A modern
stove and oven sits in the fireplace, and
towels dry on a creel that is suspended high
above it, well out of the way of activity below.
This photograph was taken in 2010.

opposite

BROOK COTTAGE, SOMERSET, IS THE
home of Christina Strutt, the founder
of Cabbages & Roses, a company that
focuses on British design and lifestyle. The
slightly crumpled fabrics give the room a
lived-in feeling, and the window seat, made
comfortable by cushions, is particularly
inviting. The table itself is loaded with
homely objects: dried flowers, a ball of
string, a box of stationery, a quilt, and a pot
of pens. As is common in cottages, the room
is small and irregular in shape. One corner
of the window shutter has been cut away to
allow it to open fully against the ceiling. This
photograph was taken in 2010.

following pages

THE BREAKFAST ROOM OF THE
Laskett, Herefordshire, the house and
garden created by the art historian Sir Roy
Strong and his late wife, stage designer
Julia Trevelyan Oman. The white and
green of the Gothic chairs echoes the
colors of the room itself and makes the
engravings on the walls, as well as the
polished wood of the principal pieces of
furniture, stand out. Fired tiles on the
floor and a rug lend warmth to the interior.
The central Gothic-style window has
no curtains and frames a view of a vine
growing up the side of the house and the
garden beyond.

THE GARDEN COTTAGE AT LEIXLIP,
Co. Kildare, was completed in 1995 and
decorated with the advice of the interior
designer David Mlinaric. A fireplace
in Kilkenny marble, rescued from a
demolished eighteenth-century building,
forms the focus of the drawing room.
On the wall is a paper with clusters of
green shamrocks. It was hand-printed
in imitation of an early nineteenth-
century design by David Skinner at his
studio in nearby Celbridge. The cottage
developed around the existing remains of
a greenhouse, shed, and garden wall. It was
designed by the Hon. Desmond Guinness,
a leading figure in the conservation of
Georgian buildings in Ireland, working
in partnership with the local architect
Basil Whyte.

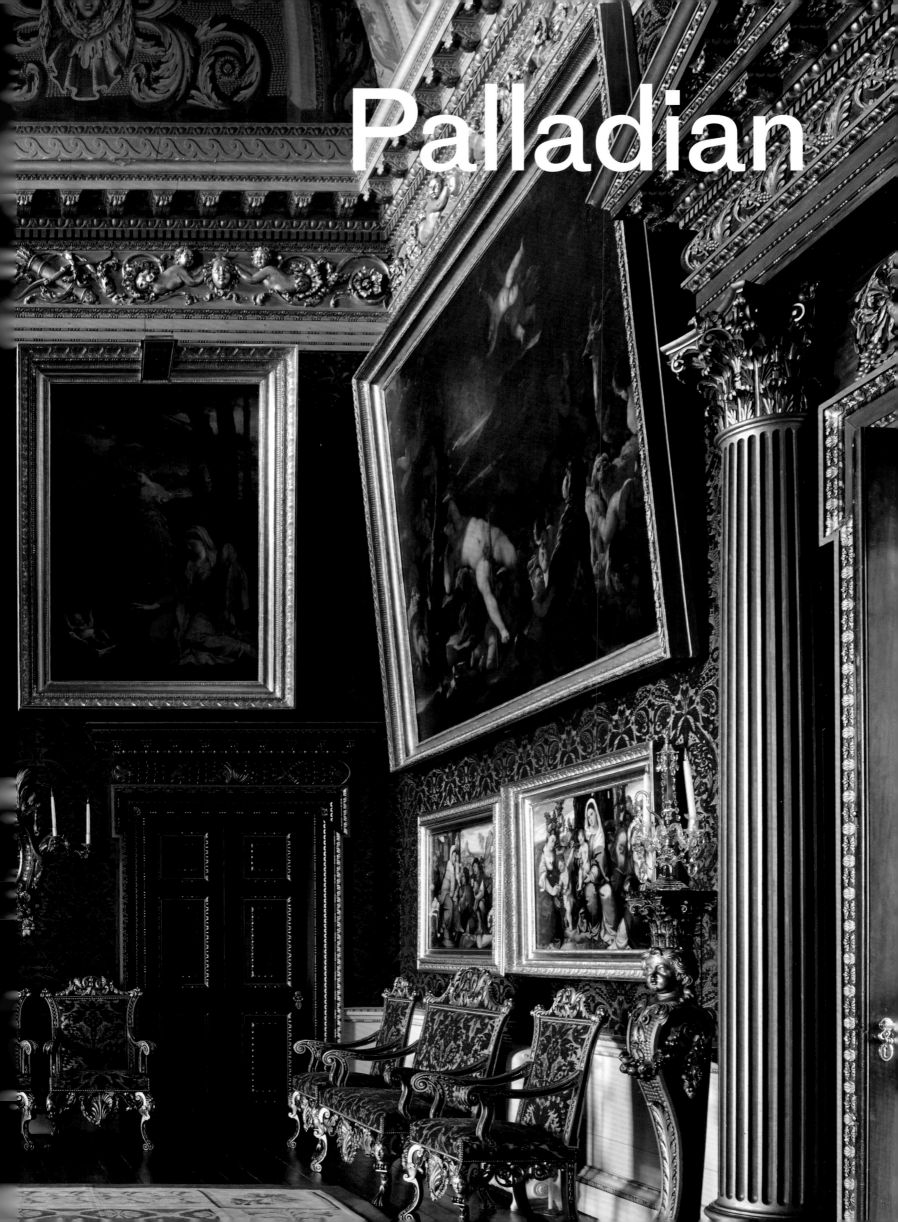

Palladian

THE PALLADIAN STYLE TAKES ITS NAME FROM ANDREA DI PIETRO, a sixteenth-century Italian who was born in Padua and, after being apprenticed as a mason, moved to Vicenza in 1524. There, by 1540, he was given the classical name Palladio by his noble patron, Gian Giorgio Trissino, a scholar and diplomat in the service of the pope. In Vincenza Palladio won renown for bestowing a Roman-inspired façade on the city's basilica, and for the next two decades worked in the city and its surrounds. From 1558, he received commissions in Venice, as well, designing churches such as San Giorgio Maggiore and country residences, or villas, in the Veneto.

Palladio's built legacy might have counted for little had he not published a technical treatise. *The Four Books of Architecture* (1570) is consciously modeled in title, form, and structure on that produced by the Classical architect Vitruvius, who lived during the first century BC. After this example, Palladio includes theoretical and practical observations, as well as drawings of ancient Roman buildings. The designs he illustrated are notable for their strict underlying geometry and internal regularity. They derive effect from a combination of symmetry, recessions of plane, and contrasting textures of masonry, including ruggedly finished stonework, termed rustication.

Both internally and externally, Palladio's architecture makes use of an identical language drawn from Classical temple design. Fundamental to this was the use of columns, either in the round or as projections from walls, termed pilasters. On the grand scale, columns might be grouped under a gable or pediment to create a portico; in miniature the same combination might form a doorcase. The columns themselves were differentiated by distinct designs to the capital and base that were grouped into the so-called five orders: Tuscan, Doric, Ionic, Corinthian, and Composite. The idea of the orders is directly rooted in Vitruvius, who describes them as expressions of the evolution of Classical design from the most primitive period.

The Four Books of Architecture has enjoyed an international reach and longevity that Palladio could never have imagined. It also won him a unique status in British architecture. To understand why, we must return to the story of the seventeenth-century architect Inigo Jones. Jones drew deeply on Palladio in his own architecture—though he knew of and used much else—and purchased and annotated a 1601 reprint of the original treatise. As part of his Italian experience, Jones also created in the Queen's House at Greenwich the first English villa, a country retreat designed in a perfect geometric form.

In the decades leading up to and following 1700, as British architects and patrons sought to create a national Roman style of architecture, they turned to Jones for inspiration. And from Jones, they looked back to Palladio. A crucial publication at this time was Colen Campbell's *Vitruvius Britannicus* (1715), a patriotic polemic examining contemporary architecture in the kingdom that sets Jones and Palladio alongside each other as models for imitation. It was a publication that effectively launched the new style: Palladianism, which treated Palladio's treatise as a foundational text for modern architectural design.

Campbell's patron, Richard Boyle, 3rd Earl of Burlington, who otherwise played a formative role in British cultural life in the period, emerged as the godfather of the Palladian style and an arbiter of architectural taste. As a matter of fact, his interpretation of Palladio was profoundly colored by Jones, after whom the style might with equal justice have been named. Burlington collected many of Jones's drawings, as well as those by Jones's pupil and son-in-law, John Webb. These were engraved and published by William Kent in 1727, Isaac Ware in 1731, and John Vardy in 1744.

Further material, including Jones's annotated copy of Palladio's treatise, were acquired by the amateur architect and fellow of All Souls College, Oxford, Dr. George Clarke. Dr. Clarke refused permission for these annotations to appear in the first full English edition of *The Four Books* published in 1721. He eventually relented, however, and they were included in the third edition of the work published in 1742. The translator in question was an Italian émigré who settled in London called Giacomo Leoni, a practicing architect whose most important surviving building, Clandon, Surrey, was destroyed by fire in 2015.

Leoni's activities as a translator and architect in London are a reminder that foreign professionals played an important role in the early development of Palladianism in the

previous pages

IN THE SUMMER OF 2013, MANY OF the paintings from the collection of Sir Robert Walpole that had been sold to Catherine the Great in 1779 were returned to his seat at Houghton Hall, Norfolk. This photograph shows the saloon of the house—its principal entertaining space— rehung as it appeared in the 1740s for this remarkable display. The interior, created by William Kent in 1725–35, preserves the original matching wall hangings and upholstery in crimson. The striking fireplace is of black and white marble. Above it hangs a painting that had been particularly prized by Walpole, Salvator Rosa's *Prodigal Son* (1651–55). The richness of this room is in stark contrast to the entrance hall (see pages 180–81).

United Kingdom. They helped connect English interiors to contemporary developments in Italy, augmenting and updating what might otherwise have been painfully dated architecture. Through their work, informed by travel as well as through such specialist publications as Rossi's *Studio di Architettura Civile* (1702) depicting Baroque architecture in Rome, Palladianism evolved and kept pace with European fashions.

Of particular importance in this regard were decorative plasterers or *stuccadori*, whose skills were used to ornament Palladian interiors. For a period English craftsmen were all but displaced by rivals from modern-day Italy and Switzerland such as Giuseppe Artari, Giovanni Bagutti, and Francesco Vassali (and their relatives). Only in the 1750s did English craftsmen reassert themselves through skilful imitation. In England stucco decoration was subjugated to the architectural logic of the particular interior. In Ireland, by contrast, stuccadori often took complete control of rooms and overwhelmed them with brilliant decoration.

Palladian interiors moved away from the dynamic gigantism of the English Baroque. In its place they emphasised proportion, geometry, and the correct use of the orders. Coffered ceilings and deep coving are also characteristic of the style. In deference to long English tradition, there remained a clear distinction between the treatment of formal interiors and those used for entertainment or domestic life. The former, notably halls and stairs, generally assume a strictly architectural form and are predominantly finished—or colored—to look like stone or marble. They were decorated with sculpture or paintings framed within the architecture. Such furniture as they contained was typically wood, without upholstery.

In contrast to these temple-like entrance halls and stairwells, the public rooms within Palladian houses were colorfully and richly furnished. Under the direction of figures such as the designer William Kent, the English domestic interior took on a new theatricality. The formal enfilade, in which the doors of multiple contiguous rooms were aligned to create an imposing vista through an apartment, gave way to a progress through rooms of varying colors and functions. As part of this effect, pictorial tapestries gave way to colored wall hangings. Paintings, meanwhile, were no longer hung opportunely but organized on the walls as an integral and planned element of the design of the room. To underline this transition, designers such as William Kent created new frames for the pictures that were in an entirely architectural idiom.

What seems surprising in retrospect about Palladianism is the degree to which it initially ignored the example of Antiquity itself. Not that this reflected a lack of interest in it. Archaeological exploration in the 1750s and 1760s began to revolutionize perceptions of the Classical past. As it did so, Jones and Palladio lost something of their cult status. Since the early twentieth century, Palladianism has enjoyed popularity once again. Architects and patrons have returned to Palladio's treatise and have tried to derive new ideas from it. What is striking about this revival is that it often looks directly to Palladio rather than the Classical world that he sought after. In this quality it shares a great deal with eighteenth-century Palladianism.

left

TO A SEVENTEENTH-CENTURY ENGLISH
audience familiar with great halls, the
entrance to the Queen's House, Greenwich,
would have come as a revelation. Begun in
1617 for James I's queen, Anne of Denmark,
by Inigo Jones, the interior is proportioned
as a perfect cube with a projecting balcony
half way up the elevation. The deeply
coffered ceiling in an Italian style echoes the
design of the marble floor, laid in the 1630s.
A cycle of paintings, Orazio Gentileschi's
*Allegory of Peace and the Arts under the
English Crown*, originally filled the ceiling.
The windows to the left overlook the
Thames and London. This photograph of
2017 shows gold flecks across the upper
walls, part of a temporary art installation
by Turner Prize–winner Richard Wright.
The architectural form and geometry of this
interior would prove to be hugely influential.

above

THIS EARLY SEVENTEENTH-CENTURY
stair at Knole, Kent, was transformed
by the 1st Duke of Dorset in the 1720s.
He commissioned the Huguenot artist
Mark Anthony Hauduroy to redecorate
this constrained space with an elaborate
trompe l'oeil scheme. The conceit is of an
interior constructed of stone with a dome
over the foot of the stair. On the wall is a
trophy of arms. Hauduroy also decorated
the Colonnade Room, visible through the
doorway. This was formerly a loggia that
overlooked the garden. The trompe l'oeil
images of giant vases and urns set into
niches are just visible. It remained popular
throughout the eighteenth century to finish
interiors that directly related to the outdoors
in stone or stone colors.

left

HOUGHTON HALL, NORFOLK, WAS BUILT
for Sir Robert Walpole to the designs of
Colen Campbell in 1722–28. William Kent
presided over the interiors, including
the entrance, or Stone Hall. As the name
suggests, the whole appears to be built and
carved out of stone. In fact, the effects are
partly created from plaster, and the cove
with deeply modeled cherubs was widely
admired by contemporaries. In conventional
English manner, the cool interior sets off
the splendidly furnished rooms beyond.
Even the hall seats are without upholstery,
a deliberate austerity. The design of the hall
with a gallery is clearly indebted to Inigo
Jones. A bust of Walpole wearing a toga and
Garter star is placed on the fireplace. Worlds
apart as this hall is from the crypt at Hexham
(see page 14, top) the interest in stone shown
here has a common origin: Rome.

following pages

CHISWICK HOUSE, LONDON, WAS BUILT
in 1726–29 and was designed by its owner,
the 3rd Earl of Burlington, a prime mover
in the Palladian revival. A contemporary,
Horace Walpole, described the building,
which was built as an addition to an older
house, as "borrowed from a well-known
villa of Palladio." Shown here is the ceiling
of the Blue Room, one of several interiors
with strong and distinctive color schemes.
The central image painted on the ceiling
probably represents Architecture, crowned
by a Corinthian capital. It's likely that the
complex geometry of the building as a whole
is suffused with meaning, one possibility
being that it was intended as a setting for
Masonic rituals, but authorities remain
divided as to how it should be interpreted.

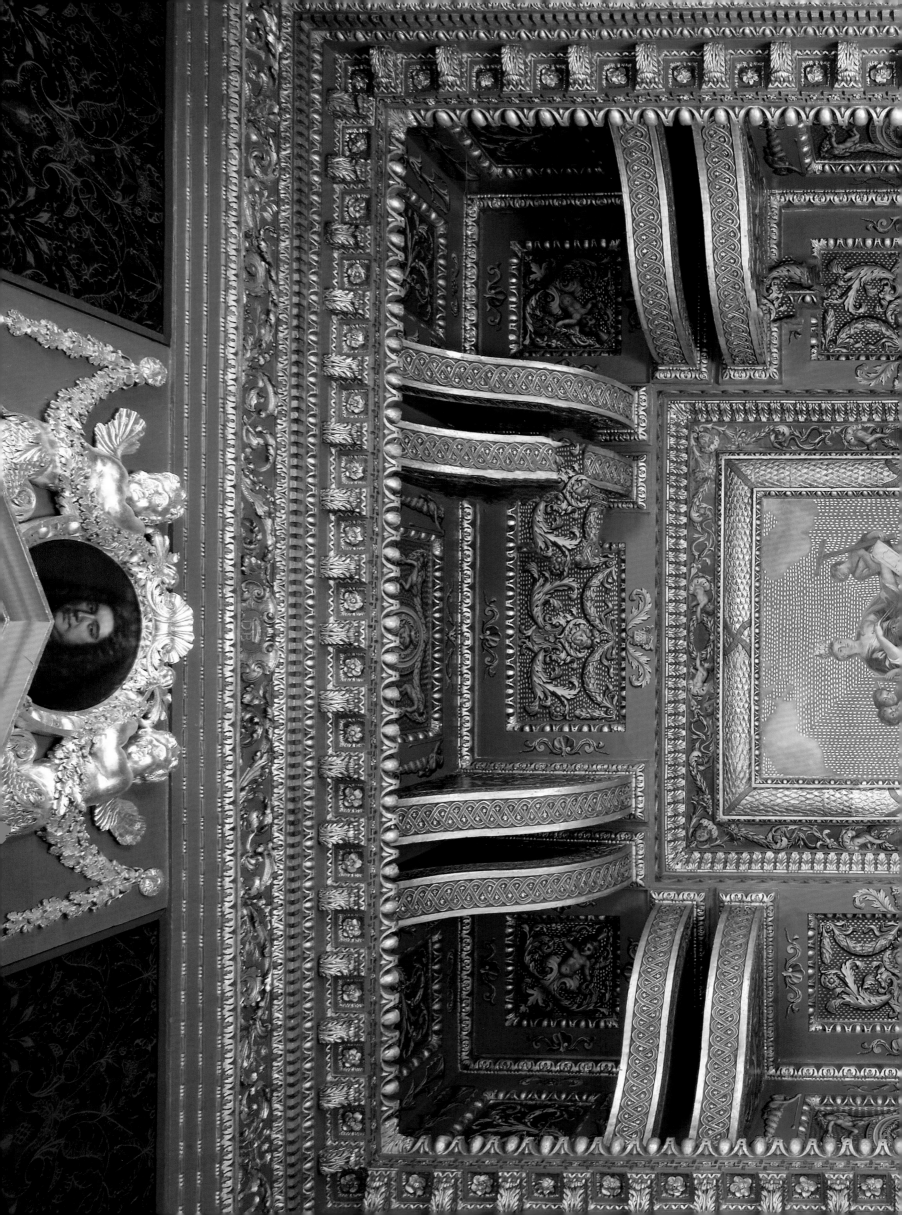

left

DITCHLEY PARK, OXFORDSHIRE, WAS rebuilt from 1720 by the architect James Gibbs for the Earl of Lichfield, and its rooms were designed by William Kent and Henry Flitcroft. In the hall the earl aimed to create a space that celebrated his learning. Over a plaster cast of Venus de' Medici in the niche are large-scale figures of the arts modeled by the Italian *stuccadore* Francesco Vassali and panels copied from the Arch of Constantine, which sits next to the Colosseum in Rome. The earl hung his own portrait in the room, which prompted John Loveday, a visitor to the house in 1734, to write, "'tis something uncommon to find a nobleman's picture in his hall, or indeed paintings of any but fictitious persons." The lights on chains are an original detail, but the seats were installed in 1738, probably to designs by Flitcroft.

above

THE MARBLE HALL OF CLANDON PARK, completed about 1729. The house was designed by the Venetian-born architect Giacomo Leoni (also the translator of Andrea Palladio into English), who used the *stuccadore* Giuseppe Artari for all the decorative plasterwork in the principal rooms. It would be a rather dull room but for the ceiling with its architectural illusionism directly inspired by Italian Mannerism. At the angles of the ceiling are figures of the cardinal virtues. Clandon was gutted by fire in 2015. It's likely that the room was cleared of most of its furniture when this photograph was taken in 1927. Chairs and carpets were scattered to fill the space.

above

THE 1730s SCULPTURE GALLERY
at Holkham Hall, Norfolk, is a deliberately
austere space intended to set off the
Classical sculpture collection of its owner,
Thomas Coke. Sculpture of this kind was
highly valued in the eighteenth century. This
interior comprises two octagonal rooms,
which were called—with self-conscious
Classicism—"tribunes," connected by a
gallery, a composition directly borrowed
from Chiswick House. Displayed in the
niche is a figure of Lucius Antonius that
was bought in Rome. The parcel-gilt
mahogany armchairs and sofas by Paul
Saunders, seen through the archway at
right, are upholstered in blue leather and
were intended to allow conversation while
contemplating the sculptures. Some of the
figures are set on the original rotating bases
to facilitate examination.

opposite

ON JULY 25, 1734, THE ARTIST
William Hogarth was elected a Governor
of St. Bartholomew's Hospital in London.
This medieval charitable foundation was
in the process of reconstruction with a new
quadrangle planned by the architect James
Gibbs. Probably in return for his appointment,
Hogarth painted the staircase of the new
building with subjects appropriate to its
charitable function: to the left is the Good
Samaritan and in the center is Christ at the
Pool of Bethesda. The ultimate inspiration
for such large-scale painting was the Baroque
decoration of the previous century by
Italian and French painters (whose work
Hogarth's father-in-law, the painter Sir John
Thornhill, emulated). Hogarth, with the help
of assistants, completed the paintings in 1736.
The gilded candelabrum, carved of wood,
is contemporary.

previous pages

THE DINING ROOM OF EASTON NESTON,
Northamptonshire, was furnished in
the 1730s by the 1st Earl of Pomfret. Its
decorative plasterwork was executed
by the *stuccadore* Charles Stanley. The
plasterwork on the walls comprises a
series of extravagant frames for paintings
depicting hunting scenes. The frame to the
extreme right is raised up to allow space for
a trophy of hunting weapons and a horn,
adding interest and movement to the overall
composition. The fireplace is made of
contrasting marbles. This photograph shows
the interior of the room in 2013, following a
major restoration of the house by its owner
Leon Max.

right

THE SALOON AT MARCHMONT HOUSE,
Berwickshire, originally functioned as
an entrance hall to the house. In 1753–57
the leading Scottish plasterer Thomas
Clayton, who had worked on a number of
projects involving the Edinburgh architect
William Adam, decorated the ceiling with
martial trophies and created the Doric
frieze just below the ceiling. In the 1910s the
Arts and Crafts architect Robert Lorimer
added much of the decorative plasterwork
on the walls, including the monograms
over the doors. The color scheme dates to
the most recent renovation of the house
since 2006 by the father and son Oliver
and Hugo Burge. A copy of a bust of the
3rd Earl of Marchmont, the builder of the
house, wearing a toga, presides over the
chimneypiece.

opposite

THE MAIN STAIR OF POWDERHAM CASTLE, Devon, is the product of two distinct periods of work. It was begun in 1754 when its magnificent plasterwork was executed by a certain John Jenkins "of Exeter" with two London assistants. Their work cost the enormous sum of £355 14s, nearly £140 more than their original estimate. Later, in the 1830s, the architect Charles Fowler filled out the Georgian decorative scheme, blocking the original windows and lighting the whole with a skylight, which is decorated with a magnificent head of Apollo in rays of sunlight. Originally, the interior would have been distempered to resemble stone. The blue is a brilliant and striking twentieth-century touch.

above right

DUMFRIES HOUSE WAS BEGUN IN 1754 for the 5th Earl of Dumfries to designs drawn up by the three Adam brothers John, Robert, and James. The house and its furnishings were saved from a sale in 2007 by the Prince of Wales. Subsequently, the Great Steward of Scotland's Dumfries House Trust has restored the interiors to evoke their eighteenth-century appearance. The work was undertaken in collaboration with Sir Hugh Roberts, former Surveyor of the Queen's Works of Art; the curator Charlotte Rostek; and the interior designers David Mlinaric and Piers von Westenholz. The North Parlor of Dumfries House, Ayrshire, was formerly a private reception room. Its silk damask was rewoven by Humphries Weaving of Sudbury.

right

THE SALOON AT CLAYDON HOUSE, Buckinghamshire, with its coffered ceiling. The fireplace was carved around 1760 in the workshop of Luke Lightfoot. It tells the story of the invention of the Corinthian order as narrated by the Roman architect Vitruvius. When a young Corinthian girl died, her nurse placed a basket of mementos on her grave and covered it with a tile for protection. A wild acanthus grew over the tile, and the resulting composition was spotted by the architect and sculptor Callimachus, who was inspired by the sight to create his new order. The nurse with her basket appears to the left, Callimachus with his dividers and a broken column to the right, and the dead maid in the center.

below

THE CENTRAL HALL OF NUTHALL
Temple, Nottinghamshire, built in 1754–57,
with plasterwork added by Robert Thomas
in 1769. Thomas was paid £1,000 for his
work. Designed by the amateur architect
Thomas Wright, the building was inspired
by Palladio's Villa Rotunda outside
Vincenza and Vincenzo Scamozzi's Rocca
Pisana. The hall is octagonal in plan and
rises the full height of the building. A
screen of columns supports a gallery that
runs around the room and is furnished
with ornate ironwork by the celebrated
Robert Bakewell. The house was demolished
in 1929 and some fragments from it were
reused at Templewood, Norfolk. The last
ruins on the site were swept away in 1966
to accommodate the M1 motorway. This
photograph was taken in 1923.

opposite

A DETAIL OF THE WHITE HALL OF HAGLEY,
Worcestershire, a house built for Lord
Lyttelton in 1754–60 by Sanderson Miller.
The interior of this entrance hall is decorated
with plasterwork and statues set in niches.
The chimneypiece, carved by James Lovell,
is supported by figures of Hercules, who is
dressed in the skin of the Nemean lion, which
also appears in the centre of the lintel, beside
a representation of his club. Just visible
above the fireplace is a panel showing a
sacrifice to the goddess Diana. It is signed by
the *stuccadore* Francesco Vassali. The house
was badly damaged by fire in 1925 but was
sensitively restored.

left

BUCKLAND HOUSE, BERKSHIRE, WAS
built in 1755–58 by the architect John Wood
of Bath, the Younger, for a Catholic patron
Sir Robert Throckmorton. He created an
octagonal chapel in the west wing of the
house, which was converted into a dining
room in 1846 when a new church was built
nearby. This photograph, taken after a
recent restoration in 2011, shows the room
as viewed from the former high altar recess
and looks westward into the room, which is
planned in the form of a Greek cross. With
its regular plan and strongly architectural
character, this is a quintessentially Palladian
room. The interior is enriched with
stone-cut sculpture and is top lit from a deep
ceiling cove. The central lantern gives the
space a visual focus.

following pages

THE SALOON OF THE PROVOST'S HOUSE
of Trinity College, Dublin, completed in
1760. The saloon extends across the full
width of the street frontage, a long narrow
room at first-floor level. At each end of the
room is a screen of Corinthian columns,
which create distinct end bays. In the main
volume of the room there is a deep coving,
visible here, that gives the room height.
The plasterwork, by Patrick and John Wall,
draws the eye upward and is wonderfully
febrile, giving the interior a sense of
movement. It is also deployed to accentuate
the architectural logic of the space, which
is unusual; Irish plasterwork is often more
freely applied and magnificently anarchic in
visual effect than its counterpart in England.

opposite

CASTLETOWN HOUSE, IN CO. KILDARE, was built by the Speaker of the Irish Parliament, William Conolly, in the 1720s. The main stair that opens off the entrance hall, however, was added by his heir in 1760. It is built of imported Portland stone, each tread cut back underneath to make the whole structure seem as insubstantial as possible. The widespread popularity in seventeenth-century England of timber staircases supported from the wall probably inspired stone structures of this kind. The polished brass balusters—an Irish peculiarity—were supplied by Anthony King of Dublin. The plaster decoration is by the *stuccadore* Philip Lafranchini. It includes picture frames and also several relief portraits of members of the family.

above

IN 1971, AFTER MANY YEARS OF NEGLECT, the fine mid-eighteenth-century house at Prehen, Derry, was rescued by Julian and Carola Peck. One of their changes to the building was to convert the former dining room into the library, seen here. The fireplace is stained from the peat that has been burned in the hearth over many centuries. The white roof has also darkened with age. The grey of the walls sets off the bright upholstery of the chairs and the gilded brackets and cornice on the bookshelves. The latter were salvaged from the ruins of Eyrecourt, Co. Galway.

HOC TEMPLVM HABITABILE ANNOS DOMINI MCM

THE ENTRANCE HALL OF MOUNT TEMPLE, Co. Wicklow, built in 1981–82, as the Latin inscription on the frieze indicates. It was designed for Dr. and Mrs. Dermot Walsh by the architect John Redmill in conscious relationship to the nearby 1750s house of Russborough. The hall is a rectangular space made circular by a screen of Doric columns supporting a low dome. On the wall are casts of Classical roundels by the Danish sculptor Bertel Thorvaldsen (1797–1838). The striking black-and-white color scheme is reminiscent of early twentieth-century Neo-Classical design by architects such as Edwin Lutyens and Herbert Baker. Though the floor looks like marble it is cut from linoleum.

following pages

THE GREAT DINING ROOM OF ST. GILES House, Dorset, turns the scars of decades of neglect into a stylish modern home, ready for everyday use. This room was originally created by the architect Henry Flitcroft in the 1740s with white-and-gold wall paneling and a two-tier fireplace. From the 1960s, the house, the seat of the earls of Shaftesbury, slid into neglect. The youthful 12th Earl of Shaftesbury, after having unexpectedly inherited the title in 2005, returned with his wife, determined to restore the place. They stabilized the interior and refurnished it but decided to preserve, rather than repair, some of the damage that had been sustained over time. The result poignantly speaks of the misfortunes of the house. Notice the ragged candelabrum cord hanging from the ceiling. The restoration work, begun in 2011, was overseen by Philip Hughes, a specialist conservation surveyor, and the contractor Ellis & Co.

above and opposite

THE TWO HALLS OF UPTON HOUSE, Gloucestershire. Upton was built in the 1750s, probably to designs by the Bristol-based architect William Halfpenny, a prolific publisher of architectural pattern books. The entrance to the house was through this magnificent, double-height hall (opposite), now used as a drawing room. Its decorative plasterwork has been attributed to the West Country professional Joseph Thomas. Corinthian pilasters rise the full height of the interior and between them, notionally suspended on rings from the entablature, are swags of plaster foliage. There are plaster picture frames and also roundels on each wall for busts. The room was originally paved in stone. In 2005 work was completed to a new entrance hall on the reverse side of the house, designed by Craig Hamilton (above). It echoes many of the details of the earlier hall, but is designed with Ionic pilasters and is vaulted. Circular openings cut through the vault light the space. The treatment of this interior suggests a later eighteenth-century style. As befits a grand entrance, the floor is laid with stone.

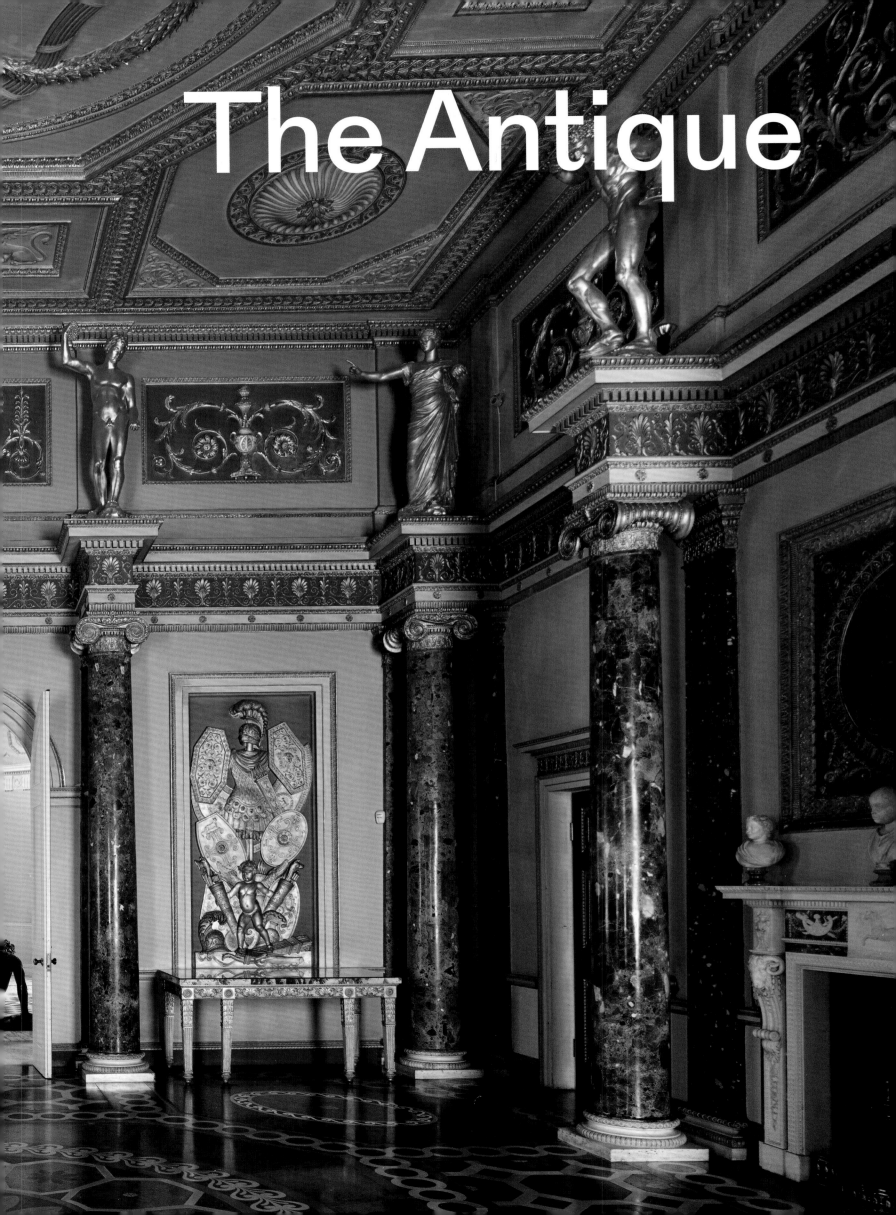

The Antique

THE RUINS OF ANCIENT ROME HAVE BEEN AN OBJECT OF FASCI-nation and wonder for centuries. As early as the fifteenth century there is evidence of art collectors exploring these ruins in search of valuable discoveries. The great artist Raphael descended into the remains of the Emperor Nero's vast palace, the "Golden House" or *Domus Aurea*, and explored the caverns, or grottos, created by the collapsed masonry. He incorporated the imagery he found there—strange and beautiful combinations of human, vegetable, and architectural forms—in his own work, most famously in the Vatican loggias around 1520. This distinctive decoration was variously termed "grotesque," after the caverns in which it was found, or "Antique," after its association with Rome. From about 1500 onward, it enjoyed a degree of familiarity across Europe.

In the eighteenth century, however, interest in this type of decoration revived once more in response to new archaeological discoveries. There had been awareness of buried remains near Naples, in the shadow of Mount Vesuvius, since the 1590s, but systematic digging of the area only began in 1748. It was not until 1763 that an inscription identifying the city of Pompeii came to light (it was mistakenly thought that an earlier inscription naming the city found in 1689 referred to the Roman general Pompey). But just as excavations in Rome were strictly controlled by the popes, so was this state-sponsored undertaking, which was overseen by King Charles VII of Naples and Spain. Every find was jealously removed and guarded, and images of the most important finds were published in luxurious volumes that were eagerly acquired as prize possessions by wealthy collectors across Europe.

The most intrepid of those collectors made their way to the sites of excavation themselves. Initially, those fortunate enough to secure permission explored the remains of Pompeii in passages dug through the site, but by the early nineteenth century substantial areas of the city were cleared. These excavations revealed a more complete picture of Roman life than anyone had believed possible. In many respects the finds were extremely challenging in that they were difficult to reconcile with the accepted view of the Roman world at that time.

Early excavations were focused on the recovery of artworks, and material of every imaginable period and style—Greek, Roman, Egyptian, and Phoenician—was revealed. Rather than see Roman culture as eclectic, however, these finds were sorted stylistically and priority was given to Greco-Roman art. Meanwhile, an aesthetic revolution took place. It was now possible to discern more accurately than ever before what Roman rooms actually looked like, how they were decorated, and even the colors in which they were painted. It was only a matter of time before these ideas were reproduced in a contemporary domestic setting.

The crucial British figure who sparked this revolution was the Scottish architect Robert Adam. After growing rich as a contractor building Highland forts for the government, Adam set off on a two-year trip to Italy in 1754. It was a journey typical of a young architect of this period, though Adam was careful to travel in the character of a gentleman. In Rome he met artists and dilettanti in the circle of the French Academy, including the artist Giovanni Battista Piranesi, celebrated both for his study of Roman buildings and his powerful engravings of architectural space and atmosphere. Adam also visited and sketched the sites around Naples. In 1757, he sailed from Venice to Split, Croatia, to examine the Roman remains there and subsequently produced a sumptuously illustrated book, *Ruins of the Palace of the Emperor Diocletian at Spalatro* (1764).

On his return home, Adam decided to leave his native Scotland—"a narrow place" as he described it—to launch his career in London. There he popularized a radically new Neo-Classical aesthetic that delighted in color, variety, and delicacy of detailing. This archaeologically inspired style was at odds with the bold architectonics of Palladian design. Nevertheless, Adam refined these Palladian forms—a process already begun by architects in the 1760s—and co-opted them in the service of his new style, which he called the Antique. It took London by storm. Very quickly Adam was busy with an enviable clutch of commissions, many of them appropriated: Adam was skillful at persuading patrons to dismiss their existing architects in favor of him.

previous pages

THE VESTIBULE OF SYON HOUSE, Middlesex, was created by Robert Adam in the 1760s. It makes spectacular use of artificial marble, or scagliola, in the projecting columns and the floor, as well as gilding. This opulent interior was inspired by the decoration of Roman palaces. Its strong colors are in stark contrast to the cool pale tones of the hall, just visible through the door. Such variety strongly appealed to Adam's wealthy and sophisticated London clients.

One reason Adam was so compelling to new clients was that he designed not only the structure of a building, but also its rooms and their decoration, including the furniture and even the fittings. Adam would lay out his designs in beguiling and beautifully finished presentation drawings. He would even harmonize the colors of the exquisite Antique detailing on his decorative plaster ceilings with carpets, upholstery, and fittings. As a result, his interiors were exceptionally coherent creations, with the style and color of the furnishings consonant with the overall design of the room.

What lent dynamism to Adam's work was his interest in movement. As he described it: "... the rise and fall, the advance and recess, with other diversity of form, in the different parts of a building, so as to add greatly to the picturesque of the composition." Adam created interiors in which each consecutive room felt wonderfully and completely distinct from the last. In late eighteenth-century London, where grand entertainment was so central to social and political life, such variety was an essential means of impressing guests. Adam's competitors were quick to follow where the market led, notably the prolific and ubiquitous architect James Wyatt, who rose to acclaim no less rapidly with his rendering in London of the Pantheon in Rome, which opened in 1772.

Assessing the nature of Adam's contribution during a lecture to students of the Royal Academy in 1812, the architect Sir John Soane spoke of a "revolution in art." He went on to observe that "the light and elegant ornaments, the varied compartments in the ceilings of Mr. Adam, imitated from Ancient Works in the Baths and Villas of the Romans, were soon applied in the designs for chairs, tables, carpets, and in every other species of furniture." It's further evidence of Sir John Soane's admiration that he bought Adam's drawings, which are still preserved at his house museum in London. Subsequent generations have been no less impressed with this style, and the Antique—which is also sometimes described simply as the Adam Style—has been imitated from the mid-nineteenth century to the present day.

A DETAIL OF THE FIREPLACE AND wall painting in the Etruscan Room at Woodhall Park, Hertfordshire. The house was built by Sir Thomas Rumbold, using the fortune he made in India, and was designed by the architect Thomas Leverton. Designs for the house were exhibited at the Royal Academy in 1777. The form of the paintings is directly inspired by Roman precedent and in particular discoveries made in Pompeii and Herculaneum. The color palette and form of the decoration is drawn from the example of Roman ceramics, which were highly prized by collectors. They were also widely imitated, most famously by the Wedgwood factory, and were enormously influential in popularizing the Antique style.

left

THIS PAINTING OF BACCHUS COMES from a set of 1540s panels preserved at Loseley Park, Surrey. It would have been characterized as "antique" or "grotesque" by Tudor viewers, terms used to describe images and decoration directly inspired by paintings found in the collapsed ruins, or grottos, of ancient Rome. By tradition, the Loseley panels are associated with Henry VIII's palace at Nonsuch and have been tentatively attributed to the Florentine Antonio di Nunziato d'Antonio, known as Anthony Toto, who worked as Serjeant Painter to the court from 1543 until 1554.

opposite

THE MARBLE HALL OF KEDLESTON, Derbyshire, forms the centerpiece of a new house built by Sir Nathanial Curzon after he inherited the property in 1758. It's a monumental interior with every surface finished in marble or stone-like colors. Curzon changed his architect three times, employing first Matthew Brettingham, then James Paine, and, finally, Robert Adam. It was at Adam's direction that the columns were carved with vertical "flutes," but he had little impact on the rest of the interior. His clerk of works was Samuel Wyatt, who went on to collaborate with his brother James in the construction of London's Pantheon. More important changes were made in the 1770s. The chests visible at the far end of the room are in fact benches created by John Linnell after the manner of Roman sarcophagi.

following pages

THE HALL OF SYON, MIDDLESEX, WAS designed by Robert Adam as part of his transformation of the house in 1762–69. It was conceived as a Roman hall, or atrium, and entered from the right. The room is decorated with Classical sculpture, including *The Dying Gaul* in bronze. Other figurative elements allude to warfare and hospitality, conventional themes in English halls. The ceiling design, which is echoed on the floor, is in the style of Inigo Jones. The plasterwork was executed by Joseph Rose. This austere room in Syon is an introduction—and a visual foil—to one of the most spectacular series of eighteenth-century interiors to survive in Britain; these rooms exemplify Adam's idea of movement.

below

IN 1763, SIX MONTHS AFTER INHERITING Newby Hall, Yorkshire, the young William Weddell set off on a tour of the continent. He returned in 1765 loaded with purchases, including tapestries from the Gobelins factory outside Paris and a substantial collection of sculpture from Italy. Weddell approached Robert Adam in 1766 about accommodating these sculptures. The result was this gallery, which culminates in a dramatic half-dome containing one of Weddell's prize possessions: a Povonazzo marble sarcophagus. This photograph, taken in 1997, shows a recent repainting of the interior. Adam's use of color is very difficult to reconstruct; he often presented patrons with more than one paint scheme

for the same design and also could depart from his original proposals.

opposite

THE GREAT ROOM AT KENWOOD HOUSE, London, was designed in 1767 by Robert Adam and decorated and furnished from 1769 to 1770. It has been redecorated since 2012 by English Heritage and furnished according to a surviving inventory of 1796. According to Adam the room "was intended both for a library and a room for receiving company." He also noted that "stucco work of this ceiling and of the other decorations is finely executed by Mr. Joseph Rose … and the grounds of the panels and friezes are coloured with light tints of pink and

green, so as to take off the glare of white, so common in every ceiling till of late … and [to] create a harmony between the ceiling and the sidewalls with their hangings, pictures and other decoration."

THE DRAWING ROOM AT BROADLANDS, Hampshire, was completed in the 1760s, possibly to designs by James "Athenian" Stuart, a pioneering figure in the revival of Neo-Classicism. The well-traveled Lord Palmerston commissioned the work and was closely involved in planning the decoration: a drawing for similar designs survives with annotations in his hand. The plasterwork is unusually bold and was executed by Joseph Rose in 1768–69. The mahogany doors were installed in 1771, and the fireplace and mirror were probably added by the architect Henry Holland in 1788. This photograph of 2012 shows recent changes to the interior by Lady Brabourne, on the advice of interior designers and partners David Mlinaric and Hugh Henry. The walls and curtains are hung in pink rep, the chairs have been reupholstered in a French fabric, and a new carpet laid in stone, green, and porphyry.

IN JANUARY 1772 THE ARCHITECT JAMES Wyatt burst onto the scene of fashion with the opening of a vast assembly room on Oxford Street in London known as—and designed in imitation of—the Pantheon in Rome (at that time still one of the largest interiors in the world). It was a project that won him numerous commissions, including work at Heaton Hall, Lancashire. This is the Cupola Room, the dressing room of then owner, Lady Egerton. It's a circular room at the top of the house with fine views. The architectural details are drawn from Renaissance Roman models—Bramante's Belvedere Court in Rome and Raphael's Loggia for the Vatican—as well from archaeological discoveries at Pompeii. According to surviving records, the painter Biagio Rebecca was paid £130 for his work in this room.

IN 1773 THE DIPLOMAT SIR JOHN Goodricke inherited a fortune through his wife and turned his attention to improving Ribston, his Yorkshire seat. He almost certainly employed the York architect John Carr, who collaborated with Robert Adam at nearby Harewood. Indeed, the splendid interiors of that house possibly inspired this interior. Some of its motifs come from engravings published in Joachim von Sandrart's *Teutsche Academie* (1768 edition). The paintings are copies of admired Italian masters and set in the wall with plaster frames. The striking color scheme dates to 1846, when the room was redecorated by Charles Moxon from London. It has since been known as the Harlequin Saloon.

below

IN 1768 LADY LOUISA CONOLLY, a daughter of the Duke of Richmond, described the pleasure of making alterations to her house in Ireland at Castletown, Co. Kildare: "All this finishing work is so very entertaining, I am as busy as a bee, and that you know is mighty pleasant." Lady Connolly decorated this room with her own hands, cutting out the prints and pasting them to the walls, a testimony to her taste and enthusiasm. Such rooms were popular across Europe in the eighteenth century, as prints—bought both loose-leaf and in collections—were relatively cheap. They were the principal means by which most people encountered celebrated buildings and paintings. This is a unique survival from the period in Ireland.

opposite

THE DINING ROOM AT CRICHEL HOUSE, Dorset. In 1772 the owner of the house, Humphrey Sturt, visited Wyatt's new Pantheon in London. He was so impressed that he immediately handed over responsibility for ongoing alterations to his house to the young architect. Wyatt sent designs for the work from London and continued to receive payments from Sturt until 1780. Building operations were locally managed, and this dining room was complete by 1776. It has recently been restored by its present owners, Mr. and Mrs. Chilton, working with the architect Peregrine Bryant, the specialist paint analyst Patrick Baty, and the decorators Hesp Jones & Co. The far door was reinstated after being discovered in the cellar of the house. The work was completed in 2015.

left

THE MARBLE SALOON AT STOWE, Buckinghamshire, was clearly inspired by the Pantheon in Rome. It was probably conceived by the Piedmontese architect Giovanni Battista Borra for Earl Temple in 1775 and completed for his nephew, the 1st Marquess of Buckingham. Its finishes are of stone and marble (or their imitations), from the Carrara floor to the scagliola columns resembling Sicilian jasper. A set of Classical sculptures were imported from Rome to fill the niches. The plaster frieze was probably modeled by Charles Peart, who also worked for the ceramic manufacturer Josiah Wedgwood. Between 2003 and 2005, Purcell Miller Tritton restored the interior. In 2009, the denuded interior was furnished with eight plaster casts of Classical sculpture (the originals having been sold in the 1920s) and tripod incense burners called *atheniennes*.

above

THE STATE BED AT OSTERLEY HOUSE, Middlesex, designed by Robert Adam in 1776. A visitor in 1788, Mrs. Lybbe Powys, described this room as "the English bed-chamber, as all the furniture is English." Her observation is correct, but a visitor might be forgiven for doubting it. In a masterful transformation, Adam took the conventional form of a four-poster bed and turned it into a fantastical and exquisite confection, with figures of crouching sphinxes, emblems of light, at each corner. The walls were originally hung with green velvet and the bed was likewise predominantly green, a color associated with fertility. The state bed chamber stands between a drawing room hung with tapestry and a dressing room, painted with Etruscan designs.

opposite

THE TAPESTRY DRAWING ROOM OF
Inveraray Castle, Argyll, in Scotland is hung
with Beauvais tapestries commissioned
by the 5th Duke of Argyll in 1785. Tapestry
lost none of its appeal or prestige in the
eighteenth century; indeed, it remained,
quite simply, the most expensive and opulent
wall covering that money could buy. Chairs
and furnishings were also upholstered with
the material. The quality of portability that
had made tapestry so useful to peripatetic
noblemen and monarchs in the Middle Ages,
however, was no longer significant because—
as in this case—it now formed part of the
fixed decoration of a room. The painting over
the fireplace is of Lady Charlotte Campbell
by John Hoppner.

above

THE PRINT ROOM AT WOODHALL PARK,
Hertfordshire, was created by a certain
R. Parker in 1782. His name is preserved
in a booklet that numbers and identifies
all 350 engravings in the room. Nothing is
otherwise known about him. Engravings

were relatively cheap to buy, and in this case
depict buildings and paintings familiar to
wealthy British travelers on the Grand Tour
across Europe. Garlands and architectural
furnishings, such as the tripods over
the fireplace, form a playful addition to
the display. The room has recently been
conserved on behalf of the Abel Smith family
by the specialist Allyson McDermott, who
has cleaned and remounted all the engravings
on Japanese lining paper. The original
ground paper color of verditer blue has also
been reinstated.

following pages, left

THE SALOON OF KINGSTON LACEY,
Dorset, was remodeled by the architect
R. W. F. Brettingham, a grandson of the more
celebrated Matthew Brettingham, after 1783.
The patron, Henry Banks, may have met his
architect in Rome, where he also collected
drawings of decorative paintings. These
drawings, which survive at the house, were
used by the artist Cornelius Dixon to paint
the vault. His work was completed in 1791 at

a cost of £288. The interior was sufficiently
admired to survive major changes by the
architect Charles Barry, who conceived the
idea of niches flanking the door in about 1840,
but the marble components did not arrive
from Venice until about ten years later.

following pages, right

WHEN SIR WILLIAM COURTENAY CAME OF
age in 1789, he celebrated by commissioning
a new music room at his seat of Powderham,
Devon, from the most successful
cosmopolitan architect of the moment,
James Wyatt. Sir William and his 11 sisters,
who are depicted in roundels on the walls,
were all clearly obsessed with music, and
this splendid interior is a monument to their
passion. Wyatt never visited the property but
work to the interior was overseen by Richard
Westmacott, also the sculptor of the superb
fireplace. The two men received payments of
£623 and £4,383, respectively, an interesting
comment on their respective contributions.
William's sisters painted the Classical
roundels inset within the walls.

opposite

THE ENTRANCE HALL OF HEVENINGHAM,
Suffolk, a house that was rebuilt to the
designs of Robert Taylor. In around 1784
the architect James Wyatt assumed the
responsibility for decorating the shell of
the building. He inserted screens of false
marble, or scagliola, columns in the long
narrow hall, reducing the central area to the
volume of a double cube. He then designed
a very unusual plaster vault to cover the
interior. It was executed by Joseph Rose
and is probably of Roman inspiration.
Just below the vault are panels depicting
weapons after the painter Piranesi. The
room preserves much of its original paint,
which incorporates subtle shading to
enhance the scalloping of the vault. Wyatt's
furniture for this interior also survives,
although regrettably it is not currently
displayed here.

right

THE GREAT STAIRCASE AT CULZEAN
Castle, Ayrshire, was begun in 1787 by
the architect Robert Adam and was still
incomplete when its patron, the 9th Earl of
Cassislis, died in 1792. It was created to link
a new sea-facing front to the castle with the
existing building, a position that demanded
it be top lit. The design was inspired in part
by the Temple of Jupiter, part of the Palace
of Diocletian at Split, which Adam surveyed
and published in 1764. Subsequent owners
of the castle warmly embraced the Adam
legacy: the 12th Earl of Cassislis created
Adam interiors in the circular saloon in the
1820s, and the house underwent further
alterations in an Adam idiom in 1877.

above

THE DRAWING ROOM OF MANDERSTON
House, Berwickshire, an ambitious Edwardian
house built by Sir James Miller, following
his return from the Boer War in 1901. It was
designed by the architect John Kinross in the
Adam style and was extravagantly furnished
by Mellier & Co. and Scott Morton Company,
based in London and Edinburgh, respectively.
The rooms are hung in primrose and white,
Sir James's racing colors. In this room the
wall hangings are *brocatelle*, a particularly
expensive material that emphasizes the
pattern, with curtains of taffeta. Curiously,
the coloring of the ceiling does not relate
to the palette used in the furnishings. This
photograph was taken in 1993 to show the
appearance of the room at night.

opposite

THE MAIN STAIRCASE OF INCE CASTLE,
Cornwall, designed in a Neo-Classical
idiom by Anthony Jaggard after a serious
fire gutted the building in 1988. It opens
downward, connecting the elevated front
door of the house—just visible in the top
of the photograph—with the rooms on the
ground floor beneath. A skylight illuminates
the space. The Doric screen at the entrance
level is infilled by large sheets of glass to
create an internal porch to the front door.
A firm called Minsterstone created the
cantilevered staircase from a compound
of ground stone and concrete, and the
wrought-iron balustrade with its elegant
S-shape supports was made by Richard
Quinnell Ltd.

above

19 GROSVENOR SQUARE, LONDON, WAS
remodeled by Robert Adam in the 1760s and
demolished in 1933. The interior underwent
important alterations, however, in the
1880s at the hands of the London decorator
Frederick Arthur. He imitated the style
of the eighteenth-century decoration so
effectively that in the twentieth century
his work was confused with that of Adam
himself. The dining room shown here, for
example, is mostly a Victorian creation.
Arthur created the far screen of columns
and also the papier mâché ceiling, which
borrows the central section from the
neighboring Derby House. Notice the
mirrored doors.

opposite

THE HEAD OF THE MAIN STAIR
at 9 Belgrave Square, London. This
broad staircase connects the principal
entertaining rooms of this large London
town house. It was built in the 1820s, part of
the wider redevelopment of Belgravia that
followed the important decision of George IV
to transform neighboring Buckingham
House into his principal palace. As part of
a major program of renovation undertaken
by Lord and Lady Ballyedmond, several
interiors in this house have been decorated
with painted schemes that were executed
in 2007–8 by Magdalen Drummond, with
assistance by Lucca Cristini, Angela Inman,
Helen Shakespeare, and Alice Williams. The
stair and entrance hall are decorated in the
Etruscan manner, with designs taken from
Robert Adam's work.

THE FIRST-FLOOR WITHDRAWING ROOM of 1 Royal Crescent, Bath, Somerset, photographed in 2014, following extensive refurbishment by the Bath Preservation Trust. This is a thought-provoking reconstruction of a 1770s interior, illustrating the sophistication and colors familiar to the wealthy at that time. Notice the fitted carpet, a fashion that the former Irish MP, Henry Sandford, the first occupant of the house from 1776, might have known before his death. Many of the carpets in the house were rewoven from designs in Brintons Archive at Kidderminster. The view from the windows is described in the Bath Journal of 1772 as "the most pleasing view of ... the whole sweep of the Crescent with the Country and Serpentine River."

IN 1988 ESMOND AND SUSIE BULMER purchased an estate at Poston, Herefordshire, with a derelict property at its heart. This was a small circular house, described as a casino, erected in about 1765 to the designs of the architect William Chambers. The Bulmers restored and extended the building with the help of architect Philip Jebb and a local building firm, Treasure and Son Ltd. of Ludlow. Shown here is the dining room, which was redecorated by their son, the interior designer Edward Bulmer. He painted the relief over the door, one of three in the room, and also designed the serving tables shown in this photograph published in 2005. Their carved and painted ornament was inspired by a pair of Adam bookcase cabinets formerly at 20 St. James's Square, London.

Grotto & Garden

THE IDEA OF COMBINING GARDENS AND BUILDINGS—THE DELIGHTS of each complementing the other—is as old as architecture itself. Such relationships, which certainly existed in Britain during Roman times, are easy to trace from the medieval period. Cloisters in both palaces and monasteries, with their covered walks overlooking gardens, offered just such a juxtaposition. From the fourteenth century, the flat leaded roofs of castles and manor houses, called "leads," began to be used for recreation. At Windsor Castle in the 1360s, Edward III had his council chamber placed at roof level. This both prevented eavesdropping and, during breaks in discussions, allowed councilors to enjoy a stroll on the rooftop and the views that accompanied it.

The tradition of using the leads in this way persisted in English architecture into the seventeenth century and encouraged the creation of spectacular roofscapes, like that at Burghley, Northamptonshire, begun in 1577. Because of their popularity, from about 1470 onward, a new type of room became popular: the prospect chamber. These rooms, tucked away at the highest level and accessible from the leads, seem to have been intended as vantage points for watching the hunt, a jealously guarded aristocratic activity. By the sixteenth century, such rooms also served as banquet chambers, used for entertainments and music. Banqueting chambers could also be freestanding buildings in gardens.

Until the seventeenth century, windows were typically composed of small leaded panes of glass, which let in the light but were not easy to see out of, making it difficult visually to unite a building with its surroundings. All that changed with the advent of sash windows and larger and better panes of glass in the 1670s. Glass-making technology has improved ever since and houses have taken advantage of the fact. This is a trend that was taken to extremes in the twentieth century with huge sheets of flawless glass in floor-to-ceiling windows, or transparent walls, that make the division between a house and its garden invisible (internally at least, since glass is highly reflective externally).

Another completely different means of relating a building to the outside world is through illusions in paint, fabric, or plaster. Rooms with gardens painted on the walls are described in Classical literature, as in Pliny the Younger's description of his villa, and they have been found in fragmentary form among the excavated remains of Roman villas in Britain. In the Middle Ages there were painted schemes of this kind, as well as tapestry representations of "verdure" or flowering meadows. To such imagery, which has never gone out of fashion, may be added both highly realistic landscape panoramas and stylized local landscapes or maps on walls.

Another kind of garden interior is the grotto. The name and the idea for these enclosed interior spaces, generally within gardens, is borrowed from Italy and first began to appear in Britain in the early seventeenth century. One of the first extant examples of a grotto is to be seen in fragmentary form at Skipton Castle, Yorkshire, dating to the 1620s. Grottos come in many forms, but there is always an association with water, whether in the form of a spring or a fountain, or through the decorative use of sea shells. Grottos are best described as fantastical spaces and in the eighteenth century were created by specialist craftsmen or, in some cases, by aristocratic women. They remain some of the strangest and most wonderful interiors in British gardens, at once bizarre and compelling.

previous pages
A STARTLING FACE MADE OF SHELLS and the bases of glass bottles from a grotto begun in the early 1990s by George Oakes. It is one of three faces at the north end of an interior inspired by the paintings of the sixteenth-century Italian Mannerist Giuseppe Arcimboldo. The face was assembled before it was affixed to the wall.

THE IDEA OF A CLOISTER—A CENTRAL garden surrounded by covered corridors or walkways—probably originated in ancient times in the Mediterranean, but it enjoyed universal currency in both palace and church architecture across the British Isles in the Middle Ages. The cloister of Gloucester Abbey, now the cathedral, seen here, was rebuilt in its present form from 1351. It was greatly admired and widely copied in monasteries across the southwest of England. Cloister walks were usually open to the garden they enclosed, but in the fifteenth century it became increasingly common to glaze these spaces for comfort in winter (the glass in the windows seen here is nineteenth century). Some cloisters in abbeys and monasteries displayed narrative cycles of stained glass, implying contemplative use.

below

THE GREEN VELVET ROOM AT STOKE Edith Park, Herefordshire, photographed in 1909. The house was begun in 1697 by the Speaker of the House of Commons, Paul Foley, and completed by his son. In 1692 the house was visited by a leading garden designer, George London. It's likely that the embroidered hangings on the walls depict the gardens as they were remodeled by him in a formal Dutch style. The embroideries date to about 1710, and it is not clear where they originally hung. The illusion is of a room transformed into a spring garden with fountains playing and orange trees laid out along the walks, some of which are set in what appear to be Chinese porcelain vessels. The house was destroyed by fire, but these hangings survived and are now at the Victoria and Albert Museum.

right

ONE OF THE BANQUETING HOUSES AT Hardwick Hall, Derbyshire, which was built by Bess of Hardwick, Countess of Shrewsbury, in the 1590s. Such spaces were used for small parties called banquets, which were intimate and superbly presented entertainments that took place after the evening meal. Banquets were often accompanied by a course of fruits and sweetmeats. This room is one of six similar chambers at Hardwick that were accessible from the flat leads of the roof. They all enjoy spectacular views, though the dense leading of the windows, with small diamond-shaped quarries of glass, makes them difficult to see clearly. Improvements in the technology of making and hanging glass for windows played an important role in opening out houses to the gardens and parks that surrounded them.

THE DAIRY OF PANSHANGER, Hertfordshire, photographed in 1936. It was designed by Humphry Repton as part of his development of the property for Lord Cowper. Dairies were functional garden buildings meant for recreational use by the mistress of the house. This octagonal room was probably begun after Lord Cowper's marriage to Emily Lamb in 1805. The marble floor, fountain, and work-surfaces are all of marble and were intended to keep the room cool. There are ceramics decoratively laid out around the room, including white creaming dishes. The fretwork ceiling creates the illusion that the room is open to the sky. An almost identical painting has been recently restored at Sir John Soane's house at Pitzhanger Manor, Middlesex. Panshanger was demolished in the 1950s.

opposite

THE BIRDCAGE ROOM AT GRIMSTHORPE Castle, Lincolnshire, is a sixteenth-century vaulted chamber that was decorated in about 1750 to resemble an exotic garden. It was described in 1769 by Arthur Young as a "breakfasting closet, which is extremely elegant; quite original and very pleasing. It is hung with fine India paper ... in the centre ... the gilt rays of a sun, the ground is prettily dotted with coloured India birds; the window shutters, the doors and the front of the drawers (let in to the wall) all painted in scrolls and festoons of flowers in green, white and gold; the sofa chairs, and stool frames of the same. Upon the whole, it is in real taste." Young's characterization of this Chinese-inspired decoration as Indian underlines how unfamiliar such exotic decoration was.

above

THIS GROTTO WAS BUILT FROM 1760 FOR the Honorable Charles Hamilton at his seat of Painshill, Surrey. It is the largest and most ambitious grotto of this period and forms part of an entire island complex on the edge of a lake. It was created by the principal specialist in the field, Joseph Lane of Tisbury, Wiltshire. Water trickles through rocky gulleys in the floor to give the illusion of an underwater cave from which the tide has just retreated. The artificial stalactites hang on a timber frame and are clad with gypsum flakes

and chips topped by feldspars, which catch the light reflected from the water. This photograph was taken upon the completion of the restoration, begun in 2012, of this astonishing interior by Cliveden Conservation.

opposite

THE GROTTO AT WIMBORNE ST. GILES, Dorset, created for the 4th Earl and Countess of Shaftesbury in 1749–50 by John Castles of Marylebone, London, who was widely employed for his grotto making skills. He even

provided do-it-yourself kits for amateurs. His office on Paddington Street was called the Great Grotto and open to the public for the cost of half a crown per person. There he provided refreshments and the opportunity for visitors to take a cold bath. The grotto at Wimborne St. Giles may have been used privately for similar activities. It comprises two rooms, the outer room being lined with flints and minerals. The inner room, shown here, was covered with exotic shells supplied by Alderman Beckford of Jamaica.

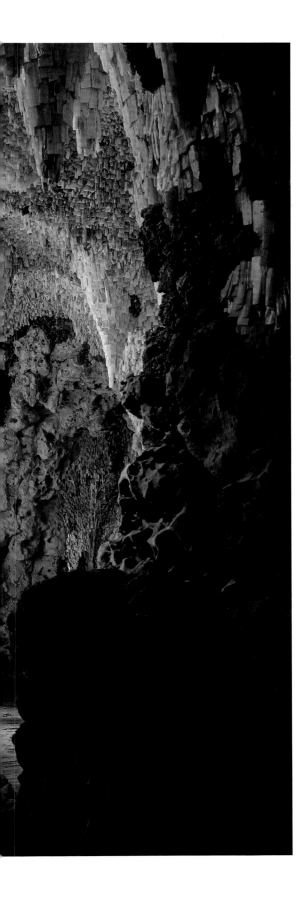

following pages

THE DINING ROOM OF DRAKELOW HALL, Derbyshire, created in 1793 by the artist Paul Sandby. The painted walls show a bower in which trellises and a picket fence—part painted, part real—define the architecture of the space. Trees lean over the vault. In the 1790s "panoramas," huge paintings representing 360-degree views of places or events, became hugely popular. It can be no coincidence that this room was created the year after the first panorama in London opened to the public. Drakelow was demolished in 1938, and a power station was built on the site a decade later. One section of this remarkable painted room—the view of Dolbadarn Castle above the sideboard at far right—is preserved at the Victoria and Albert Museum. This photograph was taken in 1907.

above

THE 1870S ROOF GARDEN AT CARDIFF
Castle, Glamorgan, in Wales is connected
to the private apartments of the building by
a spiral stair. It is surrounded by covered
walks with windows that offer wide views
across the city and countryside. All the
fittings, including the columns, the central
fountain, and the door are of bronze. So too
is the statue of the Madonna and Child by
Ceccardo Fucigna that presides over the
space. The walks are paved with mosaic and
tiles decorated with scenes from the Old
Testament accompanied by inscriptions
in Hebrew, a language that the Marquess
of Bute, the builder of the garden, was
learning in the 1870s. In the dado, which
is colored Pompeian red, are images of
animals and birds. The tiles were designed
by H. W. Lonsdale.

oppposite

THE CONSERVATORY OF BALLYFIN,
Co. Laois, Ballyfin, in Ireland was
commissioned from the Dublin-born
ironmaster Richard Turner in 1855. He
created a remarkably delicate structure.
The conservatory stands to the west of the
building, where it catches the maximum
sun. It has a large apse at both ends and is
entered through the library via a short glazed
corridor. When the Chicago businessman
Fred Krehbiel and his Irish wife, Kay, bought
Ballyfin in 2002, the conservatory was in
peril. It was dismantled and sent to England
for repair by Eura Conservation; once
restored, it was reassembled back in Ballyfin
with new glass and painted a dark green.

opposite

THE PERGOLA PASSAGE OF THE HOUSE OF Falkland, Fife, Scotland, was designed by Robert Weir Schultz but initialed by unidentified plasterers—"WGJ" and "HCL"— and dated 1894. This corridor connects the main stair with the principal bedrooms and tries to create the illusion of an indoor garden. It is lit by three domes, each with its own distinct colored glazing to suggest a different time of day: morning, noon, and evening light. The pergola itself is made from plaster and is painted with fruits and birds in a life-like manner. In the center is a text from the Elizabethan song: "Your merry heart goes all the day, your sad tires in a mile." Inlaid in the floor—but hidden beneath carpet—are tiny marquetry flowers, strewing the route to bed with blossoms.

below

THE CONSERVATORY OF 75 SOUTH AUDLEY Street in London, in 1902. It was the home of the vastly wealthy banker Henri-Louis Bischoffsheim and his wife, Clarissa. The iron and glass structure of the conservatory roof is only just visible through the tent-like folds of the fabric draped from the ceiling. Woven matting covers the floor, and the bamboo furniture and fabrics from the Orient add a slightly exotic atmosphere to the room, as does the profusion of flora. Numerous lamps imply the use of this space at night. The far wall is lined in mirrors, which reflects the back of the house and gives the impression of a much larger conservatory. This photograph was taken for *The King*, a short-lived sister magazine to *Country Life* that focussed on London.

following pages

THE KITCHEN WINDOW OF ASTHALL Manor, Oxfordshire. Because Asthall is a Jacobean house, this window with its leaded panes might be mistaken for an ancient one. In fact it was created in 1998–99 as part of the enlargement of the bedroom by architect Robert Franklin for the owner, Rosie Pearson. On a steep bank beyond the window is a box parterre designed by garden designers Julian and Isabel Bannerman. By this ingenious means, the garden is brought into the living heart of the house.

left

THIS MAP ABOVE A FIREPLACE AT ELTHAM Palace, Kent, was made of sewn leather in the 1930s by Margarita Classen-Smith. This photograph was taken in 1937. The fireplace still survives though the colors and detailing have lost their freshness. Eltham appears in the center of the map and various landmarks around it are drawn out. A wind dial is set in the top right corner. There was a revival in the depiction of maps in domestic rooms during the early twentieth century. Typically they were placed in the hall, where they would orientate visitors and display the size of the estate.

below left

THE ROUND DINING ROOM AT BIRCHENS Spring, photographed in 1938 shortly after this house was completed. A mural by the drawing master of Uppingham School, A. W. M. Rissik, depicts a fantasy of India. He was presumably a relative of the house builder, the stockbroker Cornelius Rissik. The architect was John Campbell, who trained in Munich before World War I. The round table is made of burr ash, a wood prized for its grain and patterning. The table was fixed in the room, and the glass panel at its center could be lit up from below. Lighting is also situated in the cornice that runs round the base of the shallow dome. Despite the copious lighting, each place at the exquisitely laid table is provided with its own candle.

opposite

THE TENT ROOM OF PORT LYMPNE, KENT, painted by the artist Rex Whistler in 1930. Beneath a tent canopy supported on poles are lively vistas in the manner of the seventeenth-century French painter Claude Lorrain. The room was added on to the house in the 1920s. The builder, Sir Philip Sassoon, had been a trustee of the Tate Gallery when Whistler was commissioned to decorate the tea room that today serves as the gallery restaurant. Whistler was also employed at Sassoon's house in Trent Park, just outside London. Sassoon developed a taste for Georgian art that blended well with this playful display.

THE CONSERVATORY AT DITCHLEY PARK, Oxfordshire, probably an addition of the 1930s, when the house was purchased by the MP Nicholas Tree and his wife Nancy (later Nancy Lancaster). With decorative advice from Boudin in Paris and the help of the architect Paul Phipps they created at Ditchley an interior of defining importance in mid-twentieth-century taste. Their achievement was to take the romantic and picturesque qualities associated up to this point with manor houses and transfer them to a Classical interior. The conservatory sits within a curving eighteenth-century passage connecting the main house to one of its wings. It's filled with flowers and overlooks a sunken formal garden by Geoffrey Jellicoe, who was appointed on the recommendation of Edward Hudson, the founding editor of *Country Life*.

MRS. PRICE'S ROOM AT HARRINGTON
Hall, Lincolnshire, was created in the
aftermath of a fire that gutted the house
in 1991. The owners, David and Shervie
Price, who had recently bought the place,
determined to rebuild the property. They
worked with the architect Guy Taylor and
interior designer, Christopher Nevile,
who lives at nearby Aubourn. This room
was made and installed by Oriel Harwood.

It takes the form of a bower in which the
boughs of the trees are bent and intertwined
to create the elements of the room including
the vault, the fireplace, and the central light.
The idea is borrowed from a long-standing
theory—which was popular in the eighteenth
century—that Gothic architecture evolved
in this way.

A FIGURE OF VENUS STARES OUT FROM the wall of a vaulted grotto begun in the early 1990s by George Oakes in an abandoned undercroft next to his country house. The grotto, which took twelve summers to complete, incorporates a few exotic shells of special significance. Most of it, however, is constructed using easily available materials such as flint, glass, and the shells of scallops, mussels, and limpets. The brick vaults are largely undecorated, but this makes the shells picking out the lines of the architecture stand out more clearly. Oakes worked for more than thirty years with the firm of Colefax and Fowler.

below

THE GARDEN LIBRARY
at Quenington Old Rectory, Gloucestershire, the home of David and Lucy Abel Smith. It's a free-standing building—literally a room in a garden—with a conical roof that externally resembles a dovecote. It was built in 2008 to a design by the architect Michael Gold. The work of the Scots-Polish textile artist Professor Norma Starszakowna lines the curving doors, which are open in this photograph. When the doors are open, the library turns into a backdrop for an outdoor stage. The room is heated by its own stove.

right

THE INDOOR SWIMMING POOL
at Sullingstead, Surrey, a house that was built by Edwin Lutyens in 1897 and extended in 1903. This swimming pool was created when the house was modernized after 2001 by the architect Michael Edwards. The pool has been cut into a cleft in the hillside and is therefore concealed from the main Lutyens elevations. Internally the pool is detailed in steel with a plaster vault. The structure of the façade, however, visible through the glass, is of oak and preserves the visual integrity of the Lutyens elevation. A canal extends from the pool, leading the eye out into the landscape beyond.

left

THE GARDEN LOGGIA OF SOUTH
Wraxall Manor, Wiltshire, a medieval
manor house purchased in 2005 by the
musician John Taylor and his wife, Gela
Nash-Taylor, co-founder of Juicy Couture.
They embarked on a major restoration
program with the interior decorator Robert
Kime, opera designer and director Patrick
Kinmonth, and the architect Mary-Lou
Arscott of Knox Bhavan. When the modern
kitchen was removed, this late-seventeenth-
century loggia was revealed. No windows
were added so this space remains open to
the outdoors.

following pages

THE FELLOWS' LUNCH ROOM AT ST.
John's College, Oxford, which was a 2004
extension to the Senior Common Room
designed by the architect Sir Richard
MacCormac. It takes the form of a glass box
suspended at first-floor level within a small
concrete frame, creating the illusion of a
room floating in the canopy of surrounding
trees. A deep timber and steel dado at table
level visually demarcates the lower level of
the room from the upper. There are openings
in the center of the ceiling to lighten this
naturally dark room. Oak shutters pivoted
on the concrete outer frame can enclose the
room, but when open, the eye is immediately
drawn to the enormous windows that bring
the outdoors inside.

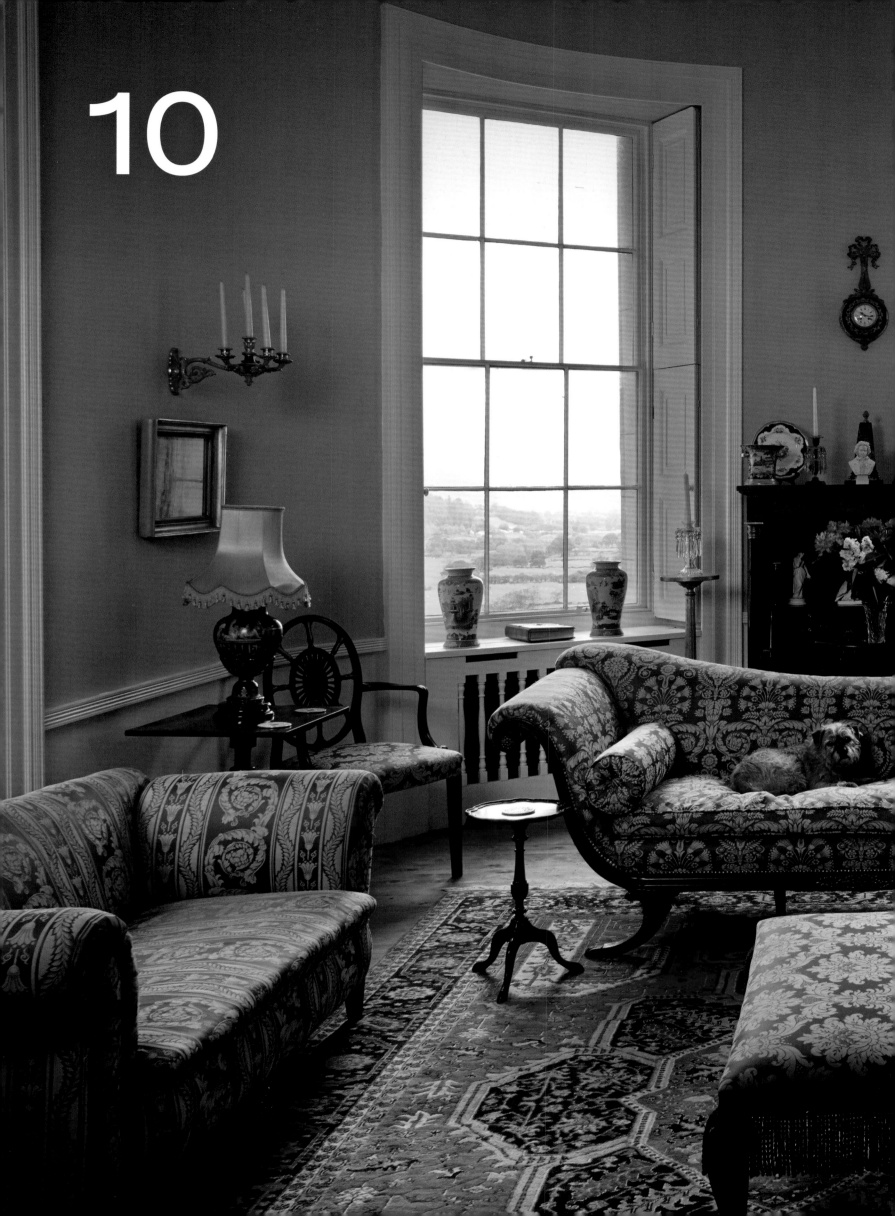

10

Regency

AT THE VERY MOMENT WHEN ANTIQUE, THE STYLE OFFERED BY Robert Adam, seemed to enjoy the highest status in British taste, the seeds of its overthrow had already been sown. An agent of this change was Robert Mylne, a brilliant young architect who studied in Rome during the 1750s and traveled to Sicily, where he studied the Greek temples of Agrigento. Mylne's career in London was launched in 1760 with his design for a new bridge across the Thames at Blackfriars. In his work, Mylne applied a more functional aesthetic to the language of Classicism, seeking to reduce the decorative vocabulary it had acquired in previous decades. His ideas were in alignment with radical theories that had been developing in both France and Italy, which posited that the fundamental laws of architecture were to be found in nature and could be expressed in forms as lowly as a primitive hut.

This movement toward rational simplification grew in popularity through the 1780s and 1790s, during which time it had a profound effect on interiors, which now displayed, for example, the broad, shallow vaults found in late Roman buildings. At the same time, it encouraged an approach to architecture that was more experimental and eclectic than paradigmatic Palladianism. For this reason, the paring down of architecture became bound up with a related but parallel development, that of a growing interest in Greek architecture. In the eighteenth century Greece remained relatively inaccessible to the West under Ottoman rule. The first accurate survey of Athenian architecture, *The Antiquuities of Athens* by James Stuart and Nicholas Revett, was published in 1764. Such studies offered students of the Antique a new source of inspiration—architecture with new orders and no arches—that had an authority of its own.

This evolution of thought and outlook took place against the backdrop of one seismic political event that compelled a reappraisal of accepted ideas across every sphere: the French Revolution in 1789. Britain watched, mesmerized, as events unfolded in France. Initially, opinion was sharply divided about whether to accept the revolution as a welcome development or not. Briefly, the new French state that replaced the monarchy advocated the idea that art should be produced in the Athenian spirit for citizens, a boost to the Greek revival. But then conflicting views surfaced about the rise of Napoleon, whose early artistic patronage through the figures of Charles Percier and Pierre François Léonard Fontaine exercised a powerful influence on Britain. Even the prolonged hostilities that ensued between England and France had an impact on art. Napoleon's invasion of Egypt, for example, offered a completely new stylistic horizon to those who were questioning the primacy of the Roman world (the revival of Gothic also received a boost at this time in Britain). As emperor, however, Napoleon's artistic aspirations took a more explicit Roman turn.

From all of this tumult there emerged in Britain a new Classical style: Regency. The term strictly applies to the period between 1811 and 1820 when the madness of King George III required that his son rule in his place. As a style, however, Regency evolved over a longer period, from about 1790 to 1830. It shared much in common with the Antique Neo-Classicisim of Robert Adam and James Wyatt, and in many regards developed from it. Screens of columns, for example, remained a popular device for articulating interior space and creating internal divisions within rooms. Early nineteenth-century Classicism, however, was more qualitatively refined and severe than Antique. It also drew ideas from a wider spectrum of material, notably Greek architecture. With less surface decoration, the play of light in interiors became enormously important, so too did the delicacy of moldings and recessions of plane. Colored light, usually a tint of amber (a color favored in false marble of the period as well), also appeared in some British Regency interiors for the first time.

In this period there took place in very specific circumstances a reassessment of the relationship between sculpture and architecture. In 1799 the 7th Earl of Elgin set off as ambassador to the Sublime Porte in Constantinople. To accompany him, he gathered—at private expense and with some difficulty—a mainly Italian entourage, who would record in drawings and plaster casts the architecture and sculpture of classical Greece. His intention, as he loved to explain to anyone who would listen, was "to improve the arts in Great Britain."

previous pages
THE DRAWING ROOM BOW OF HENDRE House enjoys spectacular views across the Conwy Valley in North Wales. The house was built in about 1802 by a local gentleman, John Edwards. It's not known if he employed an architect, but the plan and elevation resembles a *Design for a Villa* (Plate 80), published some years later in William Pococke's *Modern Furnishings for Rooms* (1811). The house had an unhappy twentieth century and by 2000 was in an advanced state of neglect. It is shown here in a photograph of 2014, following its heroic restoration over several years by Michael Tree. He furnished the interior in the Regency style, introducing appropriate furniture and fireplaces. That visible here was manufactured in China to the dimensions of its lost predecessor.

In his new role as ambassador, the Earl was responsible for sustaining British military operations in the eastern Mediterranean, which culminated in Napoleon's defeat at the Battle of Alexandria and subsequent expulsion from Egypt in 1801. He took the opportunity, however, to secure a writ, or firman, in Constantinople, directing that his workforce of copyists in Athens be given every official facility. It was by means of this document, backed by bribes and threats, that his private secretary and chaplain, Philip Hunt, removed many of the surviving sculptures from the Parthenon on the Acropolis, including what is now known as the Parthenon frieze. He acted in part to save the sculpture, shocked by the damage it was sustaining.

Elgin remained in Constantinople until 1803. Then, lured by an armistice with France, he set off for England by land. Hostilities broke out again while he was traveling, however, and he was arrested with his family and held captive in France. Happily for him, his assembled collections of antiquities had traveled by sea, and the marbles safely arrived in Britain in 1804 while he was imprisoned. It reflects his awareness of their importance that he rejected an offer, deriving from Napoleon himself, that he would be released if he sold them to the Louvre.

In 1806, the Earl finally returned home, but under a parole that ended his public career. Deeply indebted, he attempted to sell the marbles to the government. Despite enormous public enthusiasm, the government failed to act until 1816 (and by then offering much less in payment than the Earl hoped for). When they went on display in the British Museum the following year, they caused a sensation.

Hitherto, sculpture collections had by necessity been strange, eclectic assortments of pieces from a variety of dates and contexts. So much so that in the eighteenth century works of sculpture were regularly ordered by British buyers through Roman agents sight-unseen with nothing more than dimensions. With the arrival of the Parthenon frieze, however, architects, designers, and patrons were able to see for the first time how sculpture of the highest quality might relate to architecture. Suddenly, earlier collections of sculpture by comparison appeared muddled and amateur. This idea of architecture as a frame for a clear sculptural iconography would arguably have an influence even on the Gothic revival, encouraging patrons and architects to forge a connection between the two art forms.

Meanwhile, in the early nineteenth century, attention also turned to the creation of furniture appropriate to such interiors based in part on archaeological discoveries. A preeminent figure in that process was Thomas Hope, a Scottish-Dutch banker whose house in London became a display for celebrated classical sculpture and Greek vases. After opening his house to the public, he published *Household Furniture* (1807). This was a book inspired partly by the contemporary work of the Parisian architects and designers Percier and Fontaine, illustrating complete Neo-Classical interiors and their furniture.

Hope's collections were later moved to Deepdene, Surrey, a house he bought and further developed over time. His collections survived there intact until 1917, when they were sold off. The sale catalyzed a revival of interest in Hope's work and the Neo-Classicism of the Regency period. Furniture from the sale can still be seen at Buscott Park, illustrated in this chapter, and was bought up by collectors. At the same time, Regency architecture was explored as a basis for a style of modernist Classicism sometimes termed "stripped Classicism" because it eschewed the use of the orders.

In more recent years, the Neo-Classicism of the decades around 1800 has been revived more often than perhaps any other style. That's partly because its refinement and interest in light particularly appeal to contemporary sensibilities. It's also due to the continuing popularity of some of its outstanding practitioners, notably the architect Sir John Soane. Soane's house museum on Lincoln's Inn Fields in London, left untouched since his death in 1837 (at his request), remains a popular visitor attraction and an important center for the study of architecture.

THE SHALLOW-DOMED ANTEROOM AT THE base of the main staircase at Broughton Hall, Yorkshire, was created by William Atkinson as part of alterations to the house in 1807–14. Atkinson was based in Manchester and a pupil of the architect James Wyatt. The anteroom was built to connect the dining room to a new and splendid drawing room. With its shallow dome, the interior seems unusually spacious and certainly grander than a mere corridor. Atkinson's changes to the house were paid for by Stephen Tempest and his new wife, Elizabeth, the daughter of Henry Blundell of Ince near Liverpool, a celebrated collector of Classical marbles (see page 65). She inherited from her father a taste for art, travel, architecture, and collecting and actively contributed to the changes in the house.

THE DRAWING ROOM OF BROWSHOLME
Hall, Lancashire, was designed by Jeffry
Wyatt (later known as Wyatville) in 1805.
Its shallow dome is a feature characteristic
of early nineteenth-century design. Crimson
silk hangs on the walls. The fireplace was
carved in Rome and was purchased after the
English client for whom it was originally
made died unexpectedly. Wyatville's
drawings for the interior, which survive
in the house, show that the picture hang
was integrally planned with the room. It
incorporates copies of old masters as well
as paintings by such contemporary English
painters as Romney, Smirke, and Callcott.
The room forms a striking and fashionable
contrast to the remainder of the house,
which is in the Tudor style with a collection
of curiosities and antiquities.

opposite

THE INNER HALL OF BELSAY HALL, Northumberland, designed and built in a Grecian style by its owner Sir Charles Monck in 1810 to 1817. He was inspired to adopt this style by his honeymoon travels in Greece and Sicily. This photograph, published in 1940, shows the interior before it was stripped of furniture and statuary. The hall came into state care and is today managed by the nonprofit organization English Heritage. Finished in exquisitely cut stone, this soaring interior is top lit from a clerestory. At the ground and first floor levels, the screens of columns define corridors connecting the rooms; they also conceal a stair to the right. As befits their importance to the structure, the lower columns are Ionic and much larger than those above. Elegant ironwork screens with built-in light stands connect the Doric columns above.

below

THE LOWER ROTUNDA OF THE THEATRE Royal, Drury Lane, London, following its restoration in 2013 by Sir Andrew Lloyd Webber. The Theatre Royal was built in 1811–12 by Benjamin Wyatt, son of the architect James Wyatt. The upper section of this room is a domed space copied from his father's most famous interior, the Pantheon on Oxford Street (itself borrowed from the Pantheon in Rome). In the center of the room is a copy of Antonio Canova's *The Three Graces*, installed in 2013. In the corner niches are heroes of the theatrical world: Shakespeare, Edmund Keane, David Garrick, and Michael Balfe.

above

THIS STAIRCASE AT ST. GILES HOUSE, Dorset, was probably added to the building as part of a set of alterations undertaken by Thomas Cundy for the Earl of Shaftesbury from 1813. It is not an interior of great individual importance, but it perfectly illustrates the restrained elegance typical of Regency Neo-Classicism. Notice the decorative recessions of plane within the archway that create visual interest without compromising the simplicity of the whole. Also the restrained iron balustrade to the stair: the only detail on it that seems to exceed the needs of pure functionalism are the ironwork florets on each upright that give the whole visual presence.

opposite

THE ENTRANCE HALL OF OAKLY PARK, Shropshire, designed by C. R. Cockerell as part of his alterations to the house that began in 1819. The architect was about the same age as his client, Robert Clive, and like him had journeyed in the Mediterranean and the Near East. The staircase lies at the center of the house and is top lit by an iron and glass lantern. Supporting the landing are columns with distinctive Ionic capitals copied from fragments that Cockerell discovered at the Temple of Apollo Epicurius at Bassae, Greece. He also used casts of a frieze he found at Bassae and incorporated them into the decoration. Forming the newel post at the bottom of the stair is the base of a column, as if the house was built up around a ruin.

left

THE ENTRANCE HALL OF FOTA HOUSE, Co. Cork, Ireland, created by the father-and-son team of architects Sir Richard Morrison and William Vitruvius Morrison in the 1820s. This long room connects the dining room, drawing room, and library of the house; in the early nineteenth century there was a move away from the direct interconnection of rooms. This space, which punches through the vestiges of an older house, is lent visual interest by the scagliola columns, which are doubled up in the middle and applied as pilasters to the terminating screen walls. They give the interior a much deeper and grander appearance than it really has. The yellow of the columns, imitating Sienna marble, is typical of this period.

following pages, left

A VIEW OF THE TRIBUNE OF WOTTON House, Buckinghamshire, restored since 2013 by the owner David Gladstone. The original interior was created in 1820–21 by the architect Sir John Soane after the eighteenth-century mansion had been devastated by fire. It was subsequently partitioned up in the 1920s and lost within the building. Using Soane's drawings, and with Ptolemy Dean as project architect, a local team under the supervision of Michael Harrison restored the space. Harrison's team worked from the top down, recreating details where necessary, such as the winged angels at the angles of the dome, which were modeled and cast by Sarah Mayfield. The heraldic panels are on canvas and are original. They were removed in the 1920s and rediscovered in storage.

following pages, right

THE LIBRARY OF BORRIS HOUSE, Co. Carlow, Ireland, created from 1812 by the architectural team of Sir Richard and William Morrison. It is a vaulted, first-floor room furnished with bookcases made of rosewood and brass. A signature of the Morrisons is the repeated wreath in the plaster of the cornice. Borris remains the seat of the Kavanagh family, descendants of the kings of Leinster. One of the treasures of the library is a great volume—lying open on the table in the foreground—bound in red morocco and magnificently illuminated. It is the family pedigree, created at enormous expense by a herald in 1817, that purportedly traces the family tree back to 1,670 BC.

previous pages

THE SCULPTURE GALLERY AT CHATSWORTH, Derbyshire, which was restored during the life of the 6th Duke of Devonshire, who entered into his inheritance in 1818. Much of the sculpture was collected by the duke on his visits to Rome in 1819–23. Having been dispersed around the house in the 1920s, the sculpture has been redisplayed here according to the research of Professor Alison Yarrington and Charles Noble. The colored marble columns and pedestals inlaid with mosaic are in striking contrast to the neutral grey of the walls and floor. The room was described by one friend, the Countess of Mulgrave, as "more like a dream of beauty than anything in reality I ever saw … there is a glow … about it that is like a Poet's or Painter's Dreams."

above

THE ENTRANCE HALL OF WORMINGTON Grange, Gloucestershire, which was added to the house in 1826–28 by the architect Henry Hakewill. It stands between two spacious reception rooms. The top-lit lobby at the far end of the hall, beyond the Ionic screen, invites visitors into the house. It has been suggested that the Grecian quality of the design at Wormington reflects the influence of Hakewill's assistant, John Goldicutt, who had studied in Paris, was a member of the Academy of St. Luke in Rome, and published such studies of classical monuments as *The Antiquities of Sicily* (1819).

opposite

THE HALL OF BALLYFIN DEMESNE, Co. Laois, Ireland, created by Sir Richard and William Morrison as part of their remodeling of the house from 1822. Their patrons, Sir Charles and Lady Coote, worked in the spirit of their family motto, *Coute que coute*—"Cost what it may"—and turned the house into one of the finest Regency buildings in Ireland. In the center of the hall is a mosaic that was sent from Rome in 1822 by the Italian painter and designer Gaspare Gabrielli. The Chicago businessman Fred Krehbiel and his Irish wife, Kay, bought Ballyfin in 2002. With the help of Purcell Miller Tritton architects, the architect John O'Connell, and myriad specialists, they have returned the house to its former grandeur.

following pages

THE DINING ROOM AT HOLMWOOD HOUSE, Glasgow, Scotland, built in 1857–58 by Alexander "Greek" Thomson for James Couper, a paper manufacturer. Thomson never traveled to Greece, but he saw it as the model for his architecture and believed the Acropolis of Athens, before its ruin, to have been "one of the most glorious sights which the human eye has ever been permitted to behold." He was a meticulous and idiosyncratic architect. Evident here is both his distinctive framing of doors—derived from an engraving of the lost Choragic Monument of Thrasyllus—and his delight in the polychromatic stenciling of Greek motifs. This room incorporates a frieze based on John Flaxman's 1793 illustrations of Homer's *Iliad*. The fireplace is of black marble with gilded incisions.

left

THE 1780S HALL OF BUSCOT PARK, Oxfordshire, was extensively reordered by the 2nd Lord Faringdon, starting in 1934, in the Regency taste. He collected the early nineteenth-century furniture seen here, including the ebonized couch and chairs by the furniture maker Thomas Hope, which Hope made for the Egyptian Room in his London house. They are also illustrated in his *Household Furniture and Interior Decoration* (1807). An obsession for all things Egyptian swept Europe in the aftermath of Napoleon's campaign there, and the defeat of his navy at the Battle of the Nile in 1798. In the background of this room are trompe l'oeil trophies painted by Roy Hobdell in 1950. The prominent chandelier was probably designed by George IV's favorite architect, John Nash, in 1806–9.

above

A 1938 PHOTOGRAPH OF THE LIBRARY chimneypiece at 5 Belgrave Square, London, taken shortly after the house had been extravagantly renovated by Mr. Henry and Lady Honor Channon. They employed as their architects Lord Gerald Wellesley, later Duke of Wellington, and Trenwith Wills, who created a Regency revival interior that incorporated the original nineteenth-century fireplace. The cameo paintings in gold and black were executed by Michael Gibbons. Just visible in the mirror is one of the bookcases described as being of "Deepdene" type, a reference to a Greek revival house that was demolished in 1967. The predominant colors of this interior were blue, white, and pink. The library filled the front room of the first floor of the house, a position usually reserved for the drawing room.

THE ENTRANCE HALL OF BROOMHALL
House, Fife, Scotland, the seat of the Earls of
Elgin and Kincardine. The 7th Earl of Elgin,
whose diplomatic posting as ambassador
to the Sublime Porte in Constantinople
in 1799 made it possible for him to secure
the sculpture from the Parthenon, drew up
countless designs for the reconstruction of
his house, many of them on an astonishingly
grand scale. None came to fruition. The
house and its interior assumed their
present form starting in 1865. They are
clearly conceived in homage to the earl as a
collector of Classical sculpture, with casts
from the Parthenon and other antiquities.
The display is the work of the Glaswegian
architect Charles Heath Wilson. So too is
the austere Grecian detailing of the room as
a whole.

THE UPSTAIRS SALESROOM OF COLEFAX
and Fowler, 49 Brook Street, London, is
an eclectic essay in Neo-Regency design.
Founded in the 1930s by Sybil Colefax
and John Fowler, Colefax and Fowler was
one of the most influential interior design
companies of the twentieth century. This
photograph was taken in 2001, and the
company has since moved out of these
premises. Notice the tag on the cushion in
the foreground, a reminder that this is a shop
interior. The flattened vault, deep cornice,
volute brackets, and painted garlands are
all typical of the period around 1800. So too
is the treatment of the curtain (seen in the
mirror reflection) with its deep hanging
folds. Framing the doorway with a mirror
is an idea borrowed from the architecture
of Sir John Soane. It gives the illusion that
this large space opens into an identical
room beyond.

opposite

THE ROTUNDA OF BARONSCOURT,
Co. Tyrone, was created between 1836
and 1840 by the father-and-son architects
Richard and William Vitruvius Morrison.
It was strikingly redecorated by the interior
designer David Hicks for the Duke and
Duchess of Abercorn in the 1970s, part
of wider and far-reaching changes he
oversaw to the whole house. Hicks picked
out the deeply molded plasterwork in

color, including the details of the frieze,
and installed the large, round table in the
center. Hicks had the carpet woven in the
Philippines. The whole scheme is inspired
by the unusual color of the scagliola
columns. This photograph was taken in 1979,
shortly after work was completed.

above

THE HALL OF AYNHOE PARK,
Northamptonshire, was remodeled by
Sir John Soane in 1799–1804. In this
photograph of 2008 it is shown decorated
by some of the plaster-cast collection
assembled by the owner James Perkins. He
painted the interior in grey and "added a
twist of my own by painting the ceiling the
same colour as the walls. I don't highlight
architectural trim such as cornices, dados,
skirtings or door surrounds." The massive
centaur comes from a cast of the west

pediment of the Temple of Zeus at Olympia
in Greece, a carving depicting the Battle
of Lapiths and Centaurs. On either side of
the hall fireplace is a pair of eight-foot-high
candelabra columns—the originals are at
the Metropolitan Museum of Art in New
York—and a set of klismos chairs. Above
the fireplace is a cast from the Victoria and
Albert Museum of a plaque on the base of
Trajan's column.

previous pages, left

COMPLETED IN 2014, COOMBE LODGE, Berkshire, was designed by the architect Ptolemy Dean. The internal decorative scheme was largely planned by Amanda Douglas and guided by David Mlinaric. Shown here is the hall, which rises through two stories and is divided from the main stair by a thin wall punched through with multiple openings. The arrangement allows for a visual interplay of the two spaces. A dark skirting roots the interior visually and conceals wear and tear. It also contrasts with the stone-colored walls. All the detailing, including the simple staircase, evokes the work of the architect Sir John Soane, whose clean, abstract Neo-Classicism feels at once ageless and Modernist. Particularly distinctive are the delicate moldings that define all the principal features of the interior.

previous pages, right

VIEW OF A NEW ROOM AT COED MAWR, Radnorshire, Wales, designed by the architect Craig Hamilton, following his purchase of the house with his wife, Diana Hulton, in 1995. This large open space incorporates a drawing room and library, and its screen of Ionic columns is made from turned sycamore and painted to simulate red porphyry. The capitals were modeled in clay and cast in plaster by Richard Eastland. They are based on the Order of the Erectheion in Athens. Dominating the room is a fireplace of Mr. Hamilton's design that is made of Portland stone by Jamb. The ceiling is coffered and ornamented with rosettes based on those of the Temple of Vesta in Tivoli, Italy. To the right is a large, glazed casement window of bronze.

right

THE KITCHEN-DINING ROOM OF BIGHTON Grange, Hampshire, designed by George Saumarez Smith of ADAM Architecture and completed in 2015. With its spacious proportions, large sash windows, and cornice, the room feels as if it could have originated around 1800 and been converted to informal modern use. Aside from the floor, the room is entirely decorated in an attractive combination of yellow, white, and grey. This room opens through a set of double doors (framing this view) into a hall corridor. On the other side of the hall is a drawing room. All three spaces can open into one another when necessary. To take advantage of the light, the kitchen work station is set within the bay window, which looks out across countryside. The broad floor boards and wood-burning stove add warmth to the space.

11

French Revival

BRITAIN HAS NEVER REALLY FALLEN OUT OF ENVY WITH FRANCE. The relationship it had enjoyed with its larger, richer, and more powerful neighbor since the Middle Ages began to change fundamentally during the course of the eighteenth century. As Britain developed and grew as a trading power, the two became equals. Then, in 1789 came the shock of the French Revolution. There followed in its aftermath a quarter century of intermittent conflict from about 1792 to 1815 known as the Revolutionary Wars. When the Battle of Waterloo in 1815 finally brought these wars to a close in Britain's favor, the relationship between the two countries changed.

As the British resumed their habits of continental travel for leisure, they were supremely conscious that their nation was now unequivocally the most powerful and richest in the world. To emphasize the point, they briefly indulged in a vainglorious enthusiasm for all things French. These fashions particularly touched the area of London surrounding the new palace of the former Regent, George IV. He set out to create a palace worthy of the victor of Waterloo (as he perceived himself), and embarked on the reconstruction not only of Buckingham Palace, but also of Windsor Castle and his seaside villa, Brighton Pavilion.

The furnishing of the new interiors had in common an astonishing opulence, a quality underlined by the king's desire to gild almost everything. They were all rather different, however, in style. The interiors of Buckingham Palace assumed the Neo-Classical forms associated with the king's vanquished opponent, Napoleon, though burdened to the point of being overwhelmed by applied ornament. Not to be outdone, two of his brothers also began new homes nearby, York House (now Lancaster House) and Clarence House. The former was the charge of the architect Benjamin Wyatt, who also worked on an extension at Apsley House for the British commander at Waterloo, the Duke of Wellington, and at Belvoir for the mistress of the Duke of York, the Duchess of Rutland (also the real patroness of York House).

In all this work, Wyatt assumed a slightly different French style, what he described as being in the "manner of Louis XIV," or what might also be described as French Rococo. This imitated the forms of mid-eighteenth-century decoration in France and was redolent of its monarchical past, which Britain was keen to reestablish. It was also spectacularly expensive to execute, which was clearly part of the point for those wealthy enough to indulge in it. Perhaps the defining element of interiors in this style was a type of paneling termed *boiserie* that was often bought in Paris, brought back to Britiain, and pieced out with new joinery to fit its new location. Boiserie is a wainscot ornamented with elaborate flowing borders carved in the form of garlands of flowers. It could be combined with silk hangings for a richer, more dramatic effect.

These interiors adapted other distinctive French architectural forms, such as doors with flattened arches surmounted by decorative panels called "over-doors." Another characteristic was to decorate the junction where the wall meets the ceiling with a profusion of architectural or applied ornament. Furniture adopted the same febrile nature as the architecture, with every element curved, or counter-curved, and usually gilded.

The fashion for French-style interior decoration of this kind never entirely disappeared, but in the late nineteenth century, it enjoyed a revival with a particular group eager to display their wealth and taste: international bankers. Theirs was a cosmopolitan existence embracing European capitals and America, where the style was also admired and emulated. As a consequence, they were in a position to employ French architects and designers, as well as to purchase authentic French furniture. They were not interested in French Neo-Classicism but rather in the arts of eighteenth-century France.

Most celebrated of those who delighted in the style was Baron Ferdinand de Rothschild, a man rich even by the standards of his peers, who from the 1870s to 1880s established the supreme expression of this revived style at Waddesdon Manor in Buckinghamshire. The French Rococo was further popularized with the opening of the Ritz Hotel in London in 1906 by the Swiss hotelier César Ritz. It is decorated entirely in the Louis XVI style. Parisian-based design firms such as Maison Jansen kept the style alive until World War II, after which its popularity in Britain diminished. Founded in Paris by Jean-Henri Jansen in 1880, Maison Jansen became one of the most influential design houses of the twentieth century.

previous pages

THE BALLROOM OF THE SAVILE Club, 69-71 Brook Street, London. It was designed for a vastly wealthy American-born banker, Walter Hayes Burns, and his wife, Mary, after they bought the property in 1884. The architect was William Bouwens van der Boijen, who trained and worked in Paris. The original decoration of the ceiling was painted over in the 1970s, leaving flowers in urns improbably suspended amid clouds. The image on page 312 shows the spectacular staircase of this interior.

THE DRAWING ROOM OF SEZINCOTE
House, Gloucestershire, is part of a house
built from 1805 to 1811 by Charles Cockerell,
an agent of the East India Company. He
employed his youngest sibling, Samuel
Pepys Cockerell, as architect. Externally, the
house is a spectacular evocation of Indian
architecture. The interior, by complete
contrast, is French Neo-Classical in style.

Its deep cornice is decorated with hatching
to emulate the angle inside a tent. Over
the fireplace is a huge pier glass, a favorite
feature of Regency interiors. Presiding
over the richly trimmed curtains is a gilt
eagle (not visible). It stands like a captured
standard of the Emperor Napolen, testimony
to Britain's victories over the French
in India.

previous pages

THE ELIZABETH SALOON, BELVOIR Castle, Rutland, was named after the Duchess who created it. The room is furnished with *boiserie*, or wood paneling, and furniture brought from Paris. It was associated—probably incorrectly—with the house of Madame de Maintenon, the morganatic wife of Louis XIV, and cost an astonishing 1,450 guineas. The Duchess visited Paris in 1814 and blazed a trail in Britain for what became known as the Louis XIV style. To her eye it was splendid but also evoked a France before the chaos of the Revolution. The duchess encouraged her lover, George IV's brother, the Duke of York, to adopt the style in his London house. The peacocks in the cornice represent the Rutland's crest and must have been specially made for the room.

right

THE GALLERY OF LANCASTER HOUSE, London, completed between 1828 and 1848. The house was begun in 1825 for the Duke of York by Benjamin Wyatt, who was also working for the duke's mistress, the Duchess of Rutland, at Belvoir Castle. Wyatt was concurrently working on a third commission at the time, Apsley House in London, for the Duke of Wellington. All three houses were finished in the style of Louis XIV, which was drawn from printed architectural treatises. Lancaster House was sold in 1827 to the Duke of Sutherland, who hung his celebrated painting collection here. On a royal visit, Queen Victoria once quipped that she came "from my house to your palace."

THE WATERLOO GALLERY AT APSLEY
House, London, in 2015, laid out for a
banquet to celebrate the 200th anniversary
of the Battle of Waterloo. The house was
designed by Benjamin Wyatt in his Louis
XIV style and was completed in 1828–30 for
the Duke of Wellington, whom he served as
secretary in India. The room was intended
both as a setting for the anniversary dinners
the duke held to celebrate his final victory
over Napoleon, and also as a gallery for his
collection of paintings. At the core of this
collection was a set of 165 pictures from the
Spanish royal collection, which the duke
captured from the baggage train of Joseph
Bonaparte in 1813 and returned to Spain. In
1816, Ferdinand VII gifted it back to him. A
huge statue of Napoleon as Mars stands at
the foot of the stairs to the room.

above

THE QUEEN OF SCOTS'S DRESSING ROOM
at Chatsworth, Derbyshire, was renovated
in the 1830s as part of the 6th duke's
modernization of the house. The Chinese
wallpaper is hand painted and the canopied
bed is in the style known as *à la polonaise*.
It is hung with its original chintz hangings
spectacularly trimmed with tassels and has
been relined in the original manner with
blue silk. In the decades around 1800, Paris
was awash with distinctive bed designs all
named with reference either to their form,
such as the *lit en bateau*, developed by the

designers Percier and Fontaine in the shape
of a boat, or according to their height, like
the *lit à la duchesse*, which had a canopy
dome attached to the ceiling.

above right

THE SALOON OF HARLAXTON MANOR,
Lincolnshire, probably designed by the
Edinburgh-based architect William Burn
in about 1838. This spectacular house,
built by the elusive figure Gregory Gregory,
outwardly looks Jacobean or Tudor. The
interiors, however, are in a variety of

unrelated styles. This one adopts the forms
of the Louis XIV style with densely decorated
boiserie and an exceptionally deep and
richly ornamented cove. The false pelmet
and cherubs over the large central mirror
lend a theatrical touch. It's likely that the
immediate inspiration for this style, which
had by the 1830s passed out of high fashion,
was the Elizabeth Saloon at Belvoir Castle,
which is a neighboring estate of Harlaxton.

following pages, left

THE OCTAGON DRAWING ROOM AT RABY Castle, Co. Durham, created by the architect William Burn in 1843–48 for Henry, Duke of Cleveland. The room is a magnificent composite of two completely different styles. The ceiling is Jacobean in character with broad decorative moldings and a central, hanging pendant. It is overlaid, however, with French-style gilded ornament. The silk on the walls is set in intricate scrolling frames of French inspiration, as well. The outstanding textiles in this room were conserved, and in parts replaced, in 1993.

following pages, right

THE MARBLE-LINED DINING ROOM OF Waddesdon Manor, Buckinghamshire, a house commissioned from the French architect Gabriel-Hippolyte Destailleur in 1874 by Ferdinand de Rothschild in the taste of Louis XV. Forty-two guests could be accommodated at the table, which is here laid with a forest of blooms down the center after the evidence of a Victorian photograph. This room is the climax of a sequence of opulent rooms in strikingly different colors. On the walls are mirror frames from the Hôtel des Villars in Paris.

On the fireplace wall to the left (not visible) are two tapestries by Francois Boucher of 1755–78. Such was the enthusiasm of this banking family for the arts of eighteenth-century France that revival interiors of this kind were sometimes described as works in *Le Style Rothschild*.

THE BALLROOM STAIRCASE OF
69–71 Brook Street, London, now the Savile
Club. It was built by an American-born
banking couple, Walter Hayes Burns and
his wife, Mary, née Morgan, daughter of
the Croesus J. S. Morgan. They employed
William Bouwens van der Boijen to renovate
the house after they purchased it in 1884.
Though Dutch-born, van der Boijen trained
and worked in Paris. Inspired by the Hôtel de
Ville in Nancy, the dramatic stair sweeps up
to the ballroom above. Its ceiling, reflected
in the mirrored doors, was originally painted
with cupids. The blue, white, and silver color
scheme dates to the 1970s.

THE BALLROOM AT FLOORS CASTLE,
Roxburghshire, Scotland, was one of the
rooms redecorated in the eighteenth-
century French style from 1906 to 1930
by May, Duchess of Roxburghe. A wealthy
American, she was happily married to the
duke in 1903. Working with a large budget
(often in Parisian antique shops), a sharp
eye, and the help of the celebrated interiors
firm Lenygon and Morant, she worked her
way around the building, even creating a
bathroom for herself in the French style. The
walls of the ballroom are hung with Gobelins
tapestries from the *Portières des Dieux*
series. Other styles are represented here,
such as the William and Mary chairs with
their original blue cut-velvet upholstery.

THE GALLERY OF STRATFIELD SAYE
House, Hampshire, is the product of several
consecutive periods of complementary
renovation. The interior dates to about 1745,
and the numerous prints on the wall, which
are largely of scenes from Shakespeare, were
added shortly before the house was purchased
on behalf of the Duke of Wellington in 1818.
He was then serving as ambassador to France
and living in Paris after the fall of Napoleon
and purchased the property in the city that
still serves as the British ambassador's
residence. While in Paris he collected
furniture in the style of French cabinet maker
André-Charles Boulle with its tortoiseshell
and metal-inlay finishes, hence the pedestals
and cabinets here. The walls were gilded in
the 1890s, and the carpet, designed by the 7th
duke, was woven in Madrid in 1952.

left

THE MAIN STAIR OF CRAIGENGILLAN House, Ayrshire, Scotland, part of wider alterations to the house designed by Maison Jansen before 1906. With its sinuous lines and flourishes, the stair evokes the late eighteenth-century style of Louis XV and XVI. The handrail is covered in velvet. The wallpaper and paneling are original to Jansen's work, as well as the painting in the manner of Francois Boucher over the door, just visible at far right. Craigengillan preserves Maison Jansen's original design drawings, the earliest set known to have survived.

opposite above

THE DINING ROOM AT 5 BELGRAVE Square, London, part of a spectacular series of rooms created by the owners of the house, Henry and Lady Honor Channon, for entertaining guests. It was designed by Stéphane Boudin of Maison Jansen and completed in 1936. This photograph was taken soon after the room was completed in 1938. The color scheme of the room was grey-blue and incorporated many mirrors to reflect the light during evening parties. Even the surface of the table is mirrored, and the chairs were silvered for effect. Inspiration for this room came from the Hall of Mirrors in the Amalienburg, an exquisite hunting lodge that was built on the grounds of Nymphenburg Palace near Munich by the French-trained architect Francois Cuvilliés in 1734–39.

opposite below

LADY BAILLIE'S BEDROOM AT LEEDS Castle, Kent, was designed by Boudin in 1927–29. It's a simple interior but spacious with little surface decoration. The blue paneling has been carefully distressed to bring out the grain of the wood, and the bed is specially designed in the style of Louis XIV. Lady Baillie used this room as her office. Boudin worked intensively on his visits to the castle and used Lady Baillie as a translator between the French specialists he brought with him and the English men executing his designs.

12

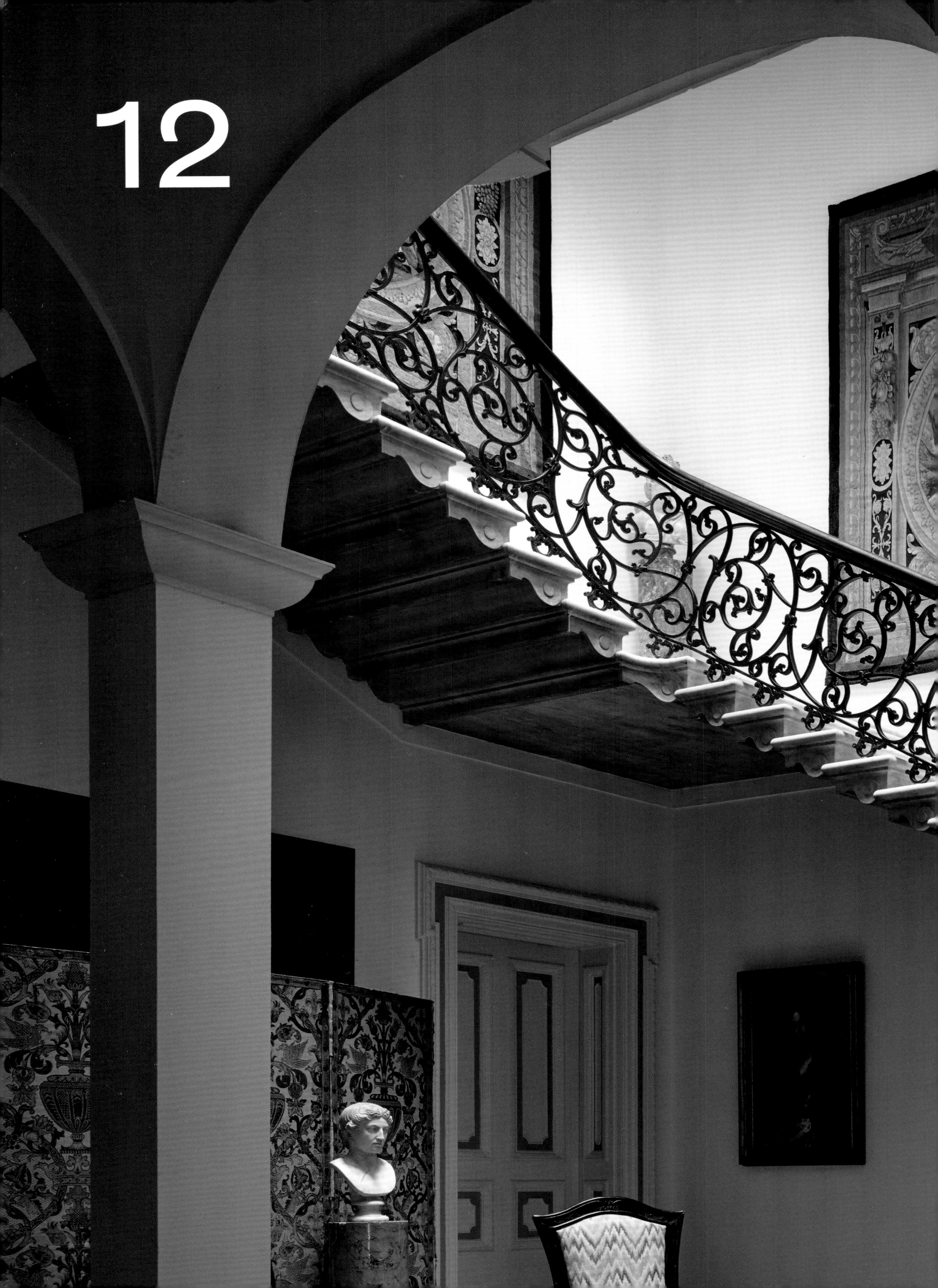

Italian Palazzo

IN THE 1830s THE BRITISH BEGAN TO FALL IN LOVE WITH LATE medieval and Renaissance Italy. The ancient Roman world still held a powerful appeal, but to a nation that had fallen under the spell of its own medieval history, it seemed only natural to seek the same in Italy. The growth of the railway network throughout Europe, meanwhile, played an important role in facilitating travel. Florence became a particularly popular destination, and one manifestation of this was the adoption of Florence as a name for British girls born in the city (such as Florence Nightingale). Venice also attracted growing numbers of visitors.

The British traveled to both cities in search of art. In Florence they saw the riches of the city through the eyes of the sixteenth-century writer Vasari. His *Lives of the Artists* offered an extremely partial narrative of Florence as the crucible of European artistic culture. So important was Vasari's account that it formed the intellectual structure for Britain's national collection of art in London, the National Gallery, founded in 1824. The British also identified with the medieval mercantile culture of Florence with its international financial interests and wealthy families. In this regard, the career of Lorenzo di Medici in particular became an object of interest and seemed to anticipate the lives of modern British merchant bankers. Indeed, for this reason a generation earlier the Liverpool banker, collector, and abolitionist William Roscoe even wrote and published a biography of Lorenzo in 1796 and one about the Medici Pope Leo X in 1805.

British visitors to Venice could engage in similar games with history. They might, for example, romantically imagine themselves as heirs to the city's maritime greatness, as did the celebrated critic John Ruskin in his introduction to *The Stones of Venice* (1851–53), a hugely popular and important guidebook to the city. Vasari paid little attention to Venice, but its art had been admired in Britain since the purchase of the Gonzaga collection by Charles I in the 1620s. No less important was the influx of Venetian paintings through art sales. After the French Revolution, the extraordinary collection of the Duke of Orleans was sold off in London and brought to Britain all the paintings by Titian—perhaps the most consistently admired of all old masters—that still remain in the country today.

Italy had long experience in the management of the international art market, and it was quick to adapt itself to new tastes. The closure of religious institutions during the Revolutionary Wars from 1789 to 1815 made available large quantities of art that agents collected for foreign purchase. Some of these sale collections were given names to imply respectability and long family ownership. One such was the Lombardi Baldi Collection purchased in Florence by the National Gallery in 1857, and another was the Camuccini Collection bought in Rome by the Duke of Northumberland in 1854. For those in pursuit of unobtainable masterpieces of the Renaissance, meanwhile, there were expert copyists who could furnish complete collections for rich tourists to ship home.

The same forces that contrived to make Italian Renaissance art popular with the rich also contrived to shape the training of contemporary artists. Of particular importance was the example of Raphael, who was held up by Vasari not only as the culminating genius of the Renaissance (along with Leonardo da Vinci and Michelangelo), but as an example for future artists to follow. As a consequence, the study of Raphael in particular came to dominate the formal training of artists. So suffocating did some British artists find this that, one group, inspired by John Ruskin, set about imitating the art of Raphael's predecessors and founded the Pre-Raphaelite Brotherhood in 1848.

Small surprise that in tandem with this desire to collect, imitate, and reimagine Italian art there should develop an interest in the Italian domestic interior. That interest in Britain was kindled by one particularly prominent building in the capital, the Travellers Club on Pall Mall in London, begun in 1829. The commission properly launched the career of the architect Charles Barry, later celebrated for his oversight of the new Houses of Parliament, which he rebuilt in a Gothic style from 1840. To a public confronted in the late 1820s by the extremes of Greek Revival and Gothic architecture, the Italianate style was a welcome alternative. It was monumental but in architectural terms relatively austere (not dependent, therefore, on costly detailing). It was, however,

previous pages
THE STRIPPED-CLASSICAL STAIRCASE hall of the Italian embassy at No. 4 Grosvenor Square, London, designed in the 1930s by the architectural practice Wellesley and Wills. The stair is cantilevered and top lit by a skylight. Its wrought-iron balustrade is patinated to resemble bronze. The internal framing arcade, borrowed from Italian palace design, is duplicated on the floor above. On the walls is a series of seventeenth-century tapestries depicting the seasons and hours. They were designed by Lorenzo Lippi and woven in the Medici workshops in Florence.

capable of magnificent decorative effects. As one contemporary critic put it, the new club succeeded in "reconciling the seemingly antithetical qualities of richness and simplicity."

The Travellers Club essentially took the form of a Florentine palazzo. Its internal focus was a central courtyard rising the full height of the interior. In Italy, such spaces are typically open to the sky, but at this club the walks are glazed over in a concession to the damp English climate. This creates a comfortable circulation space in the heart of the building with a staircase to one side. The main rooms are spacious but understated in architectural terms. All the interior walls, including those of the hall, are plastered, a contrast to the stone finish used in some country house halls. The principal rooms have internal bays demarcated by pilasters.

The Italianate style introduced by the Travellers Club subsequently enjoyed wide popularity in Victorian Britain. Its simplicity made it very adaptable, as is testified by the countless terraces, clubs, country houses, town halls, and even factories in this style that have survived to the present. It also helped that the royal family joined in the fashion with the extraordinary villa created for Queen Victora and Prince Albert on the Isle of Wight at Osborne from 1845. This was designed by Thomas Cubitt, who also used the style in the many terraces he developed across Belgravia in London.

Ironically, a byproduct of the style—and one which made it suitable for use in so many architectural registers—is that it revived an interest in and admiration for the Renaissance architect Palladio. The advantage from the point of view of nineteenth-century architects was that the Italian revival could therefore adopt grand Classical forms very easily without a jarring change of style. In the Travellers Club, for example, the one room that has a flourish is the library. It's ornamented with a screen of columns and a plaster copy of the Phygalean Marbles from the Greek site at Bassae; here the Italian Renaissance blends seamlessly with archaeological Neo-Classicism.

While British patrons constructed Italianate buildings and voraciously collected Italian art of all kinds (or created imitations of it), the furniture of the domestic interiors within these buildings was generally of a different character. In the Travellers Club, for example, Barry designed furniture that was entirely appropriate to an English country house of the period, though with some concessions to exotic taste, such as a spacious ottoman on which club members could recline.

Since the nineteenth century, Italian Renaissance architecture has occasionally continued to exercise an influence on the British interior. That's true in the context of villas but also in the particular circumstances of the 1930s, when it was hoped by some that the Classical tradition could adapt itself to serve contemporary building needs through a particular process of simplification and reduction. So-called stripped Classicism made a promising beginning, but it never took root. In Britain, at least, the palazzi of Venice and Florence are now evoked more for their romantic and historical appeal than anything else.

above

THE GALLERY OF THE CENTRAL HALL OF the Reform Club, London, designed by the architect Charles Barry in 1837. It follows the neighboring Travellers Club in assuming the form of an Italian palazzo. This hall with its enclosing galleries is the centerpiece of the design and looks like an inner courtyard, or *cortile*, except it has a roof. Unlike the Travellers Club, a relatively modest building, the Reform is palatial. Barry's two clubs instituted a fashion for Italian design in Britain that enjoyed popularity in buildings of every scale, from country houses to urban terraces.

opposite

THE MAIN STAIR OF BALLYWALTER PARK, Co. Down, Ireland, is part of a house built by the Belfast architect Charles Lanyon for the cotton magnate Andrew Mulholland in 1846–52. The house is designed in the Italian Renaissance manner made popular by Barry's Travellers Club of 1832. Its main rooms are hung with an unusually fine collection of copies of Italian Renaissance and Baroque paintings, as well as Neo-Classical furniture made on the estate. The staircase, by contrast, is a purely architectural space and the setting for sculpture. Just visible to the right is one of three plasters in niches by one of Ireland's best-known nineteenth-century sculptors, Patrick MacDowell.

THE DINING ROOM OF ALNWICK CASTLE, Northumberland, was remodeled in the 1850s by the Duke and Duchess of Northumberland. In 1849 the duke commissioned the architect Anthony Salvin to transform the castle. Soon after he traveled to Italy, where he met the archaeologist and classicist Luigi Canina. Together with his assistant, Giovanni Montiroli, Canina produced drawings for the interior apartments of Alnwick in the style of a sixteenth-century Roman palace with deeply coffered ceilings of timber and fireplaces, like this one flanked by full-length figures. To furnish the interiors, an Italian craftsman was brought to England to train a team of joiners. In 1856 the duke bought the Camuccini collection of Italian old masters and hung them at Alnwick. The green silk on the walls and upholstery are the result of a recent restoration.

previous pages, right

THE DINING ROOM OF LOCKO PARK, Derbyshire, with its coving and ceiling painted by A. Romoli, an Italian artist living in London at the time. This historic house was extensively reordered from the mid-1850s by Henry Stevens, an architect based in Derby. His patron was William Drury-Lowe, who traveled widely on the continent and made at least three long visits to Italy in 1839, 1852–53, and 1862–64. As a mark of his affection for Florence, he named one daughter after the city. He also collected fourteenth- and fifteenth-century Italian art voraciously. The new interiors of the house were intended to accommodate this remarkable collection. Romoli assisted with hanging the pictures.

above

THE DRAWING ROOM OF ASHRIDGE House, Hertfordshire, was transformed by the architect Sir Matthew Digby Wyatt in 1860 for Lady Marian Alford, who acted as chatelaine of the property from the 1820s until 1888. She was born in Italy and clearly delighted in its architecture and art, creating this Roman palace interior. On the ceiling is a copy of Guido Reni's *Aurora* fresco. The original was painted for a garden building, or casino, in Rome in 1614 and commissioned by Cardinal Scipione Borghese. The Pavonazzo marble doorcases are unusually bold for an interior space and rise the full height of the room. In one long wall are two Carrara chimneypieces supported on sculpted male figures, or telamons, by Mark Rogers Jr. When originally completed, the walls of the room were covered in crimson damask.

opposite

ST. CYPRIAN'S CHAPEL, UGBROOK HOUSE, Devon, was a private family chapel for the Catholic Clifford family that was originally built in the 1770s by the architect Robert Adam. This photograph was taken from the family pew, which is directly accessible from the first floor of the house. The family had close ties with Cardinal Weld and spent a great deal of time in Rome during the early nineteenth century. Acting as his own architect after his inheritance in 1858, the 8th Lord Clifford internally adapted the building with a new Lady Chapel and baptistery. It was converted into a public Catholic church when these works were completed in 1866. The panels of marble around the high altar, the austere Classical detailing of the elevations, and the central dome, all additions by the 8th Lord Clifford, speak of Roman influence on the reordering of the interior.

IN 1874 THE 3RD MARQUESS OF BATH employed John Diblee Crace from a dynasty of London decorators to transform the state rooms of Longleat House, Wiltshire, into a vision of fifteenth-century Italian magnificence. Shown here is the State Drawing Room, the most expensive of the rooms, for which he paid the vast sum of £1,132 in 1887. The Marquess had first visited Italy in 1854 in a journey that took him to Rome, Florence, and Venice, where he then served as "ambassador extraordinary." While there he commissioned Antonio Caldara to copy paintings by Paolo Veronese and Giovanni Battista Zelotti in the Library of St. Mark's in Venice for use in the ceiling at Longleat. Hung on the walls are Venetian and other Italian paintings he collected on his travels.

left

A 1908 PHOTOGRAPH OF THE SALOON AT Clumber, Nottinghamshire. This seat of the Dukes of Newcastle was rebuilt after a fire in 1879. Its interior resembles the courtyard of a sixteenth-century Italian palace with an elaborate marble floor. As in the case of such London clubs as the Travellers and the Reform, this space was glazed over as a concession to the English weather. It can be no coincidence that the architect of the house was Charles Barry Jr., the son of the architect who designed these clubs. The Duke was only fifteen when the house was built by his trustees. The statue is Thomas Banks's *Thetis Dipping the Infant Achilles into the Styx* (1789). Clumber was demolished in 1938.

below left

THE MARBLE HALL OF GOSFORD HOUSE, EAST Lothian, Scotland, completed in 1891 by William Young for the 10th Earl of Wemyss. It's enclosed by lofty galleries and top lit, like the internal courtyard of a sixteenth-century Italian palace. The upper gallery is entered by a huge double stair carved with the date 1890 in Roman numerals. Its openings are tripartite and comprise a central arch flanked by rectangular openings, a form possibly borrowed from the eighteenth-century work done to the house by Robert Adam. The interior makes extensive use of marble and alabaster.

opposite

THE MAIN STAIRCASE OF WESTONBIRT HOUSE, Gloucestershire, is Italian in form: it comprises straight flights of steps that are accommodated within a barrel-vaulted well. In a concession to English taste, the stairs are of wood rather than stone. To the sides are deeply cut balustrades and the vault is coffered. The stair survives complete with its original embossed blue-and-gold wallpaper, in imitation of stamped leather, supplied by Thomas Kershaw. It communicates between the bedrooms on the first floor and a long corridor. The house was built in 1864–74 by Lewis Vulliamy, a pupil of the architect Sir Robert Smirke, and member of the famous clock-making family. The building is eclectic in style, combining Tudor, Flemish, French, and Italian interiors.

following pages

THE SALOON AT BUSCOT PARK, OXFORDSHIRE, is a 1780s interior transformed in the 1890s by the addition of a cycle of Edward Burne-Jones's paintings, depicting the *Legend of the Briar Rose*. The four pictures in the cycle were painted over a period of twenty years and were exhibited to great acclaim in London in 1890. Alexander Henderson, later 1st Lord Faringdon, purchased the set for the drawing room. Soon afterward, Burne-Jones visited the house while staying at Kelmscott with his friend William Morris. He provided the frames in a sixteenth-century Florentine style and added the narrow panels that lie between them. The effect is of an Italian Renaissance *studiolo*, or study. In 1995 the room was refurbished by Alidad to mark the centenary of its creation.

above

IN APRIL 1934 THE ITALIAN AMBASSADOR declared his new embassy at No. 4 Grosvenor Square "the most beautiful of all the foreign embassies" in London. Shown here is the ballroom, designed by Wellesley and Wills, the architectural partnership of Lord Gerald Wellesley, later Duke of Wellington, and Trenwith Wills. It has a low, vaulted ceiling in an austere Neo-Classical style that was referred to as stripped Classicism. The English chimneypiece of around 1770 was probably introduced in the 1930s. The room is hung with a set of eighteenth-century armorial tapestries from the Uffizi Gallery in Florence. There are pier glasses made in Rome around 1780 and an Aubusson carpet of about 1870.

opposite

EYFORD HOUSE, GLOUCESTERSHIRE, is an Edwardian house built to the designs of the architect Guy Dawber in 1911–12. The dining room, formerly the garden hall, is a modern interior, however, and its Venetian scenes were painted by Penelope Reeve before 2004. The trompe l'oeil represents the landmarks of Venice in broadly correct relationship to one another, with the Doge's Palace to the left and Santa Maria della Salute to the right. Painted on the central window blind, or shade, which is pulled down for evening parties, is San Giorgio. Venice continues to exercise a particularly strong emotional hold on British affections.

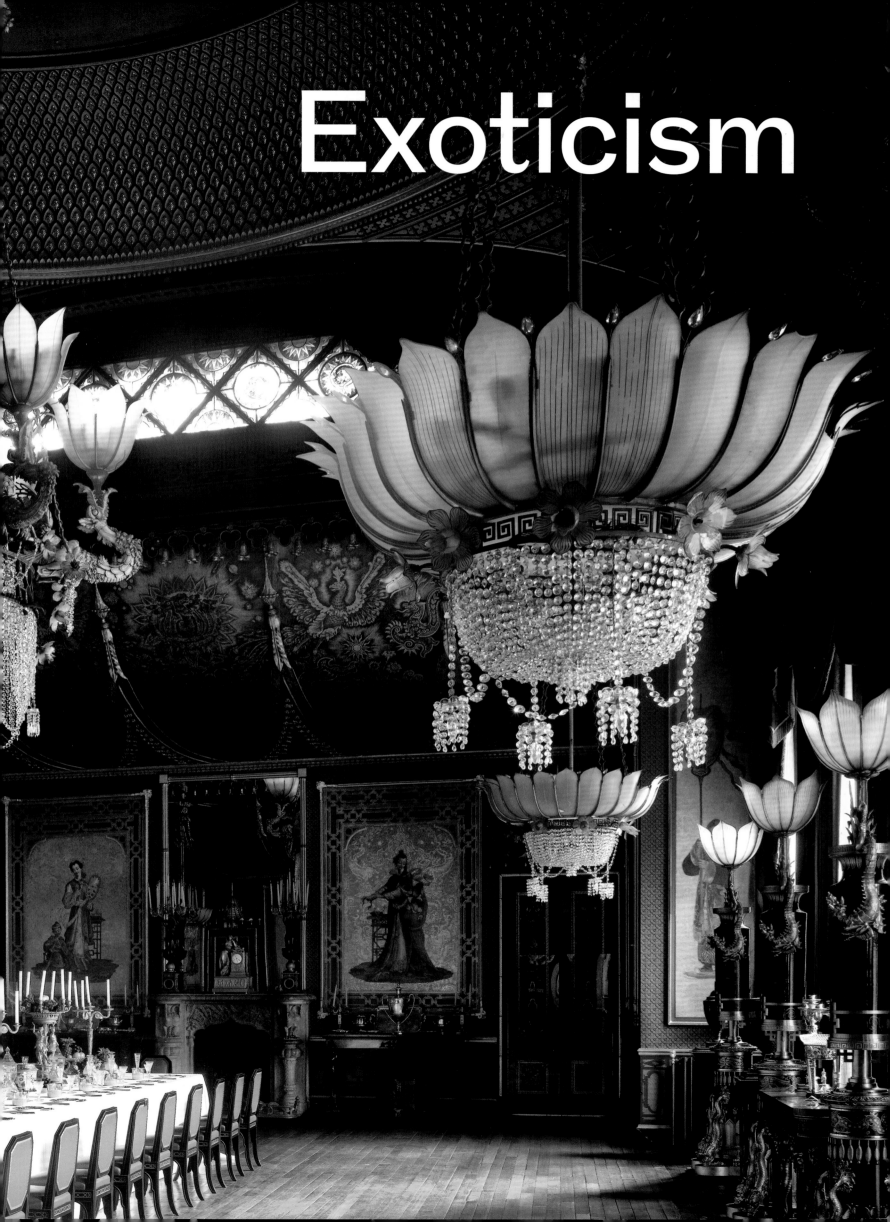

13

Exoticism

IN THE CEASELESS SEARCH FOR NOVELTY THAT CHARACTERIZES
so much of the history of fashionable interior decoration, the exotic is an easy hunting
ground for striking new ideas. An exotic object or room might be defined as something
that is neither expected nor at home, nor even readily comprehensible to its audience,
yet that succeeds in inspiring curiosity or admiration. They often include items imported
from other countries. Frequently, the most successful exotic things are embraced and
become part of the vernacular. Such was the case with chintz, which—if the writer Daniel
Defoe is to be believed—was popularized as an import from India by Queen Mary after
1688 and became a mainstay of both British clothing and interiors.

There is no obvious beginning to the importation of exotic objects or fabrics into
Britain. As early as the ninth century, the body of St. Cuthbert was recorded as being
wrapped in silks variously identified as being from Byzantium, Syria, or possibly China.
Painted depictions of cloth hangings in medieval wall painting schemes make it clear
that this was no isolated example. Nevertheless, these objects were precious because
they were rare and remarkable, not because of their particular origins. Admiration for
intrinsically inexpensive objects because of their place of origin is a British sensibility
that began to develop in the late seventeenth century and coincide with Britain's rapidly
expanding mercantile interests. By the eighteenth century it was well established.

While Georgian visitors to public buildings and country houses naturally recognized
the exotic when they saw it, many of them had no idea what they were actually seeing. To
someone who has never left Britain, and who had no access to any reliable information
about India, China, or Japan, distinguishing what came from where was impossible. Over
time the use of the exotic in British interiors has grown steadily more literate and sophisticated. Increasing ease of international travel and trade over the last two centuries has
made all but the most ingenious expressions of exoticism seem commonplace today.

previous pages
THE BANQUETING HALL OF THE
Brighton Pavilion, Sussex, created
by John Nash in 1817 for the Prince
Regent. Coleridge's celebrated poem
Kubla Khan was published in 1816, just
before the creation of this astonishing
room. On the walls are silvered panels
in the Chinese style by Robert Jones.
The chairs are modern reproductions
of the originals. There was originally
an Axminster carpet on the floor.

opposite

DITCHLEY PARK, OXFORDSHIRE, WAS rebuilt to designs by the architect James Gibbs from 1720 for a discerning patron, the Earl of Lichfield. The earl furnished many of the rooms well into the 1730s with the help of Henry Flitcroft. His work includes the completion of this room, formerly a bedroom, hung with velvet bought in Genoa for the fabulous sum of about £292 in 1738. Its pattern is clearly inspired by representations of Indian deities, but, whereas typical depictions of these figures have complementary implements in opposing hands—a bow in one hand and an arrow in the other, for example—here, the design is reversed to show two corresponding bows. The fireplace is by the London sculptor Henry Cheere, who submitted bills for this and other work amounting to £402.

below

THE ALCOVE IN THE CHINESE ROOM OR Boudoir at Claydon House, Buckinghamshire, which was part of the house remodeled for Ralph Verney, 2nd Earl Verney, between 1757 and 1771. This spectacular feature, carved in the 1760s by the London carver Luke Lightfoot, was the setting for a day bed for tea drinking. A Chinese tea party is actually depicted in the plaster under the canopy. The alcove was probably inspired by a 1762 engraving in William Ince and John Mayhew's *Universal System of Household Furniture*. The color scheme was devised by John Fowler who worked at the house in 1956–57 and again in 1973–77. It has been shown accurately to evoke some aspects of the original color scheme. The divan is modern. This photograph was taken in 2003.

following pages

THE DRAWING ROOM AT STANWAY HOUSE, Gloucestershire, is dominated by two canopied day beds in the Chinese style. Their design is derived from the 1754 and 1759 editions of the richly illustrated pattern book by the celebrated furniture maker Thomas Chippendale titled *The Gentleman and Cabinet-Maker's Director*, also commonly known as *The Director*. This publication offered designs for furniture in many different styles, and it allowed patrons to indulge in a vast array of tastes, be they French, Gothic, or Chinese. Dressed with curtains and flowers, day beds were used by women to receive guests. These two examples were made for the Palladian house at Amisfield Park, East Lothian, built by the Honorable Francis Charteris, later the 7th Earl of Wemyss, and his wife, Lady Katherine. Francis and Lady Katherine were both subscribers to the first edition of *The Director*.

THE MUSIC ROOM OF THE BRIGHTON
Pavilion, Sussex. After the defeat of
Napoleon at Waterloo in 1815, the Prince
Regent directed his favorite architect, John
Nash, to remodel his seaside retreat at
Brighton. Nash reported that he was asked
to bestow on the enlarged building "an
Eastern character, and by its picturesque
effect to fix the attention of the spectator . . ."
He excelled at his task with this opulent
interior, created in 1819, which was intended
for evening entertainments, during which
the stained glass was to be externally lit
by flaming torchères. The walls are of red
canvas simulating lacquer and adorned
with Chinese landscapes partly taken from
William Alexander's *The Costume of China*
(1805). This room has been restored after
fire and storm damage in 1975 and 1987. The
original chimneypiece and organ are now in
Buckingham Palace.

following pages

THE ARAB HALL OF LEIGHTON HOUSE,
London, was built in 1877–81 to the designs
of George Aitchison to accommodate
Frederic Leighton's magnificent collection
of Islamic tiles and ceramics. Leighton
trained as an artist and studied in Germany,
Italy, and France. He enjoyed enormous
popular acclaim and in later life became
celebrated for his depiction of Classical
subjects. In 1895, less than a month before
his death, he became the first British artist
to be elevated to the peerage. This room
became one of the most celebrated in
Victorian London. Several artists of this
period had exotic rooms created to lend
glamour to studio visits. This photograph
shows the interior subsequent to its
restoration in 2008, when cream paint
applied in the 1970s was removed and the
interior regilded.

left

THE MOORISH BILLIARD ROOM AT NO. 12
Kensington Palace Gardens, London, in 1971. It
was designed by Matthew Digby Wyatt in about
1866 for the owner of the house, Alex Collier.
Wyatt was a friend of Owen Jones, whose book
The Grammar of Ornament (1856, and still in
print), is arguably one of the most influential
design sourcebooks ever produced. It explores
Islamic patterns, as well as those in nature. The
Moorish style enjoyed particular popularity in
smoking rooms and billiard rooms in the late
nineteenth century. These were both exclusively
male preserves. The remainder of the house was
done in an Italian Renaissance style, which makes
this room more impactful.

below left

THE EASTERN ROOM AT SOUTH LODGE,
Rutland Gate, London, as photographed in 1902 for
the short-lived sister publication of *Country Life*
called *The King*. The room was created for John
Allan Rolls and his wife, Georgiana, Lord and Lady
Llanggattock, in 1883 by the decorators H. & J.
Cooper. She was celebrated as a collector, though
it is likely that this room—because of its Islamic
theme—was her husband's preserve. The fabric
stretched across the ceiling creates the impression
of a tent, and the floor is almost entirely covered in
exotic furnishings, cushions, and carpets. No less
profuse is the array of ceramics and metalwork.
The massive throne to the right of the stairs clearly
has a special provenance.

opposite

THE MUSIC ROOM AT MONSERRATE PALACE,
near Sintra, Portugal, part of a house built by
Francis Cook, whose fortune derived from textiles.
Cook married an Anglo-Portuguese merchant's
daughter and purchased this estate in 1863. Using
the London architect James Thomas Knowles,
who had previously built warehouses for him,
Cook created a fantastical villa palace in the
Gothic style to accommodate him on his annual
visits to Portugal. The music room was conceived
as a Hall of the Muses with sculpted busts of nine
Muses in roundels and an additional seven Pre-
Raphaelite sprites to make up the required number
of sixteen. This extraordinary space is inspired by
the Music Room at the Brighton Pavilion.

following pages

THE CEILING OF THE ARAB ROOM, CARDIFF
Castle, Wales, one of the last interiors designed
by William Burges before his death in 1881 and
completed in 1882. Cardiff Castle, which Burges
remodeled for the fabulously wealthy Marquess
of Bute, is largely a Gothic revival building. The
inclusion of this spectacular ceiling demonstrates
the architect's belief that the medieval spirit lived
on outside Western Europe: "At the present day,
the arts of the Middle Ages have deserted Europe,"
he wrote in 1862, "and are only to be found in the
East. Here in England we can get medieval objects
manufactured for us with pain and difficulty, but
in Egypt, Syria, and in Japan, you can buy them
in bazaars."

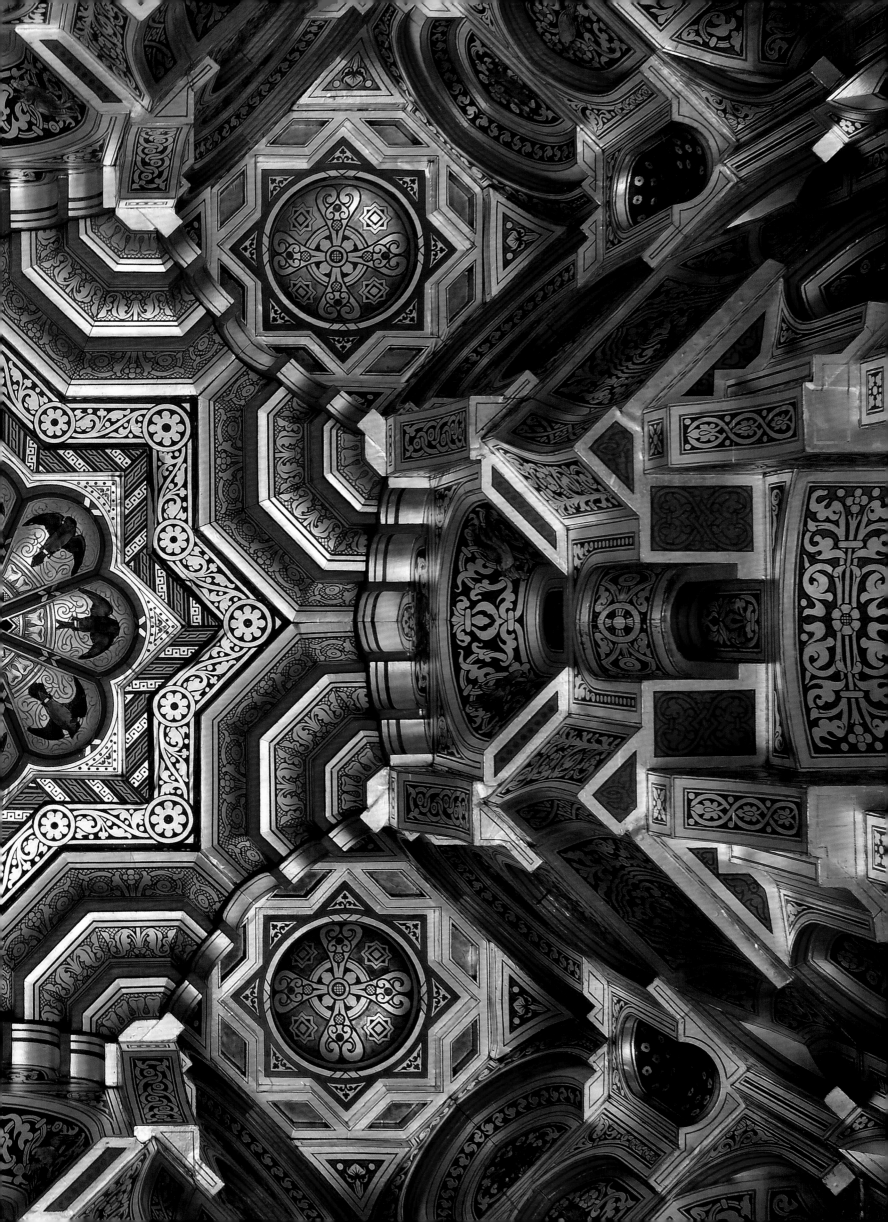

A BEDROOM AT NEWSTEAD ABBEY, Nottinghamshire, with Japanese paneling, paintings, and furniture. It was probably created in about 1900 by Miss Ethel Webb, who also created a very early Japanese garden at Newstead from 1899. She imported plants and stone lanterns for the garden (and possibly also a gardener), so it is likely that the furniture for this room was specially bought for the room in Japan. The late-nineteenth-century fashion of all things Japanese is famously satirized in the comic opera *The Mikado* (1885) by Gilbert and Sullivan. Its lyrics play on the imagery of birds and landscape that feature so prominently in this interior.

opposite

THE CENTRAL DOMED HALL OF Debenham House, London, designed by the architect Halsey Ricardo in 1905–6, a partner of William de Mogan in his renowned ceramic business. The house was built for Ernest Debenham, owner of the eponymous department store, who reputedly commissioned the architect— who was also a friend—with the words: "I want a palace and I want you to build it for me." According to family tradition, the mosaic decoration of mythological scenes, plants, and birds was added at the behest of Debenham. They make the interior strongly resemble a Byzantine church. The mosaics were executed by Gaetano Meo in 1912–13 using tesserae supplied by Salvati of Venice. The mosaics include roundel portraits of the Debenhams and their eight children.

above left

THE DRAWING ROOM FIREPLACE OF
Port Lympne, Kent, was designed by Philip
Tilden with paintings by Josep Maria Sert
in 1918–20. The paintings were part of a
decorative scheme in black and gold (now
lost) covering the entire room, depicting
France being attacked by Germany in World
War I but triumphing in the end. Even to an
enthusiastic writer who described this room
for *Country Life* in 1923, it wasn't entirely
clear how elephants, or their decidedly
exotic riders in the manner of Tiepolo, fitted
into that narrative. The subject, however, is
no coincidence: this room was the setting

for discussions in 1920 between the British Prime Minister Lloyd George and the French government, including the Marshal Ferdinand Jean Marie Foch.

opposite below

A CHINESE DINING ROOM AT 11 Montagu Place, designed by the artist and playwright Edward Knoblock. The room was photographed for a 1931 article in *Country Life* describing the revival of Regency design, a movement in which Knoblock played a leading role. Not surprisingly, this photograph was never

published. However, it points to the degree to which rooms within the same fashionable London house might be decorated in completely different styles. This added to the delight of guests as they moved between contrasting rooms of great splendor. Notice the Neo-Classical cornice of this room, a detail from the original nineteenth-century interior that survived this Chinese makeover.

above

THE DRAWING ROOM OF THE DEANERY at Durham with its hand-painted Chinese

wallpaper, which was added to the room at some point between 1911 and 1938. The Deanery was developed from the cannibalized remains of the original house built for the medieval Priors of Durham, which dates back to the eleventh century. Indeed, this room, remodeled many times over the last millennium was once the "great room" of the priors. The Chinese paper gives the illusion that the room opens up into a landscape of elegant trees filled with beautiful birds. Such wallpaper designs are highly prized and have been widespread in Europe since the eighteenth century.

opposite

LADY IRENE ASTOR'S BATHROOM AT HEVER
Castle, Kent, designed by Godfrey Bonsack.
It is a 1970s symphony in pink. The matching
pink fabric of the walls, curtains, and ceiling
is decorated with golden fleur de lys and is cut
to suggest a tent. All the bathroom fittings are
in gold, including the table with its legs and
beading shaped like bamboo, the rope towel
rail, and the faucet. The mouth of the tap is in
the form of a swan, a Bonsack leitmotif found
elsewhere in the bathroom. The bath itself is
of plastic, then still an object of luxury. It is
decorated on the outside to match the wall (as
is the latrine). Flowers line the windowsill in
a specially constructed wooden trough lined
in lead.

above

THE POOL HOUSE OF A NEO-EGYPTIAN
house called Sphinx Hill built in the 1990s on
the banks of the Thames, in Oxfordshire, by
the architect John Outram for Christopher
and Henrietta McCall. It's a consciously
modern house that celebrates the McCall's
love of Egypt and its culture (Henrietta is
an Egyptologist). The pool house is strongly
colored, as is the whole building both
internally and externally. Here, light blue
columns with gilded palm capitals give way
to lighter green walls and the garden beyond.
Meanwhile, the surface of the vault above the
pool—in fact a plastic membrane—echoes the
deep tones of the water, suggesting an infinite
depth above and below the room.

below

THE EGYPTIAN ROOM AT STOWE HOUSE, Buckinghamshire, created in about 1803 as part of a ground-floor entrance to this huge house. The interior has been restored since 2012, using early drawings, descriptions, and the evidence of the fabric. The original room was an extraordinarily early piece of Neo-Egyptian decoration and followed immediately upon the publications of Egyptian antiquities by French academics accompanying Napoleon's army, specifically Vivant Denon's *Travels in Upper and*

Lower Egypt (1803). The interior had a sanded finish intended to resemble the bare stonework of an Egyptian tomb. The lost altar and paintings have been recreated here, the latter by the artist John Maddison. The crystal sphere above the doorway to the left is part of an attempt to light the room.

opposite

THE OLD CHAPEL OF CAPHEATON HALL, Northumberland, a house built in the seventeenth century, now holds stock for the lifestyle brand of Eliza Browne-Swinburne, known as ibbi. It is not a designed space or one created for domestic living, but the nature of the objects stored here from around the world—and in particular from India and Africa—has an exotic appearance. The house was left derelict after it was requisitioned during World War II, and the efforts of three generations of the family have returned it to occupancy at last. This photograph was taken in 2017.

14

Arts and Crafts

"THE ARTS AND CRAFTS MOVEMENT," EXPLAINED THE ARCHI-
tect C. R. Ashbee in 1908, "began with the object of making useful things, of making them well and of making them beautiful; goodness and beauty were to the leaders of the movement synonymous terms." What he omits to add is that it was at first driven as much by social concerns as aesthetic ones. Its leading advocates shared a revulsion for industrialization, in part for its dehumanization of workers, but also because, in their eyes, it emasculated creativity. In this regard they were reacting against what they perceived as the clutter of poorly designed objects that filled the late Victorian home. It was to clear this away that the evangelist of the movement, William Morris, famously exhorted: "Have nothing in your house that you do not know to be useful or believe to be beautiful."

The movement had deep intellectual roots, and part of its inspiration came from the Gothic-revival architect A. W. N. Pugin. In his book *The True Principles of Pointed or Christian Architecture* (1841), Pugin argued that good architecture was founded on "true principles": that form should express purpose; that structure should be legible; that materials should be apt to their purpose and decorated in a manner appropriate to their qualities. To Pugin's mind, buildings designed by such principles, and when created by "a pious Christian" architect, were possessed of integrity or "honesty." That honesty extended to craftsmen, who needed to invest themselves in every stage of the making process (unlike specialized factory workers). The result was a process of manufacture in which there was a direct correlation between the beauty of the object and the manner in which it was made. In other words, an object was imbued by its means of manufacture with social and moral quality.

As Britain emerged as the greatest (and first) fully industrialized nation in the world in the 1850s, even those unsympathetic to Pugin began to draw similar conclusions. The most influential was the celebrity art critic John Ruskin. In his view, industrialization, or the mechanization of the creative process, and the specialization of labor that accompanied it, crushed the soul: "It is only by labour that thought can be made healthy, and only by thought that labour can be made happy." He also believed that the source of all true beauty was nature itself. Ruskin began a movement that sought to dignify, by and through nature, both the craftsman, or laborer, and his or her labors. It was believed that this process would naturally improve standards of design in Britain, which Ruskin and others felt had become inferior not only to those of other European countries but even to undeveloped nations, where the specialism and hierarchies of industrial production were unknown.

The crucial figure who transformed the ideas of Pugin and Ruskin from a theory into a living reality was the designer William Morris, the lynchpin of the Arts and Crafts movement. Morris came from a wealthy family and studied at Oxford before joining the practice of the Gothic-revival architect William Street and moving to London with the firm in 1856. Wherever he went, Morris established friendships with individuals who would become enormously influential: at university he befriended the painter Edward Burne-Jones, and while training, he met the architect Philip Webb. Then Dante Gabriel Rosetti, a co-founder of the Pre-Raphaelite Brotherhood, a group of artists who rejected the idealization of art, an idea that had been introduced, they believed, by the artist Raphael.

Through Rosetti, the painter Ford Madox Brown joined Morris's circle. It was Brown who suggested they establish a company that focused on the design of home interiors. Collectively, Morris and his circle enjoyed considerable expertise in the manufacture of furniture, stained glass, and painting. The new firm was founded in 1861, but did not acquire its familiar name of Morris and Co. until 1875. It expanded by stages into the creation of wallpapers and fabrics, with Morris abstracting the designs of flowers and foliage in conformity to Ruskin's idea that all true beauty derived from nature. Morris was a brilliantly successful businessman, but he also had a proselytizing zeal for his work. He wanted everyone to be able to enjoy beautiful things. As he expressed it in a public lecture in 1877, "I do not want art for a few, any more than education for a few, or freedom for a few."

THE SUMPTUOUS INTERIOR OF Watts Chapel stands in the cemetery at Compton in Surrey. It was consecrated in 1898 but the complex iconography, molded in gesso and picked out in brilliant colors, was not completed until 1904. The design of the chapel was inspired by the Church of the Holy Sepulchre in Jerusalem, and the work of construction was overseen by Mary Watts, wife of the artist G. F. Watts. Locals were encouraged to help decorate the interior and took lessons in modeling. From these informal classes was born the Compton Potters' Arts Guild.

The central difficulty that Morris and his circle encountered was that, although they aimed at universal improvement, the only people who were prepared to pay for Morris and Co.'s brand of simplicity and beauty were the wealthy. Sir Lowthian Bell, a friend and an extremely generous patron of both Morris and Webb, famously related the story of how he had once come upon Morris walking and talking excitedly. When he asked if anything was wrong, "he [Morris] turned on me like a mad animal—'It is only that I spend my life in ministering to the swinish luxury of the rich!'" He was lucky to have patrons who would indulge him in such outbursts. Nevertheless, the social dimension of his art remained hugely important to Morris, and in later life he became a committed socialist.

Numerous artists and architects involved in the Arts and Crafts were no less serious about the social role of their profession. Many of them chose to train as artisans and endeavored to use their own hands as much as possible. They encouraged others to do the same, establishing workshops for cottage industries such as weaving among the poor and then managing the sale of the product, often through London shops or exhibitions. Some helped organize communes or funded social projects. Others went in search of and collected folk culture, whether songs, stories, or objects to ward off evil. Some of these initiatives may sound awkwardly patrician today, but they had a clear logic at the time.

From the 1870s, the rural economy was in decline and the countryside, its life and rural traditions, looked vulnerable (as indeed they proved to be). The sensibility of the Arts and Crafts movement was to preserve the traditions as best they could and record what could not be saved for future generations.

While the Arts and Crafts remained a movement that—to the discomfort of its advocates—primarily served the prosperous, it nevertheless served them extremely well. It emerged at a moment when domestic life in Britain was undergoing enormous upheaval. In the late-nineteenth century home ownership was on the rise, and the railway network (and later the motor car) allowed for a freedom of movement previously unimaginable. It was possible, for the first time ever, to commute from the countryside to work in the city, or to visit a friend for lunch or dinner, and return home—all in the same day. Formerly impoverished rural areas close to major cities now began to flourish as they became desirable places in which to live and build a comfortable, modern house. The ideal for those who could afford it was for a modestly sized house with rooms where small groups of friends and family could be entertained, and a decent garden. In short, what we would now think of as a home; a concept formulated in its modern sense during the late nineteenth century.

It was precisely this prosperous new market of "home" builders who found in the Arts and Crafts the answer to their dreams. The Art and Crafts created buildings that looked to the forms and materials of their locality; that celebrated the beauties of nature; and that were capable of accommodating the new conveniences of modern living. Crucially, too, it was a style that was as happy to transform an existing cottage, byre, or castle into a modern house as it was to build anew on a green-field site. That's because the Arts and Crafts cherished local culture and repurposed buildings, even modest ones; they spoke of history, craftsmanship, and integrity or, more simply, Pugin's "honesty." For all these reasons, the Arts and Crafts produced more masterpieces of domestic architecture than any other style in British architectural history. It also gave birth to *Country Life* magazine. With its emphasis on high-quality printing and wide ranging interests spanning history, craft, architecture, and the joys of life in the countryside, *Country Life* is an exemplary product of the Arts and Crafts.

The legacies of the Arts and Crafts movement are many and varied. One of the most important is the conviction that a person's character can be shaped by their living environment. No less important is the idea that patina, wear, and age are qualities to be cherished. Expressed another way, that history—in the form of ancient buildings—is worth preserving and loving back to life. Finally, that craftsmanship has real value and, in and of itself, imbues things with quality. The truth of these ideas has been contested in some quarters. Nevertheless, through them, the Arts and Crafts movement continues to exercise a powerful influence on modern design and living.

left

PHILIP WEBB WAS PERSUADED TO oversee the renovation of Naworth Castle, Cumbria, in 1868. As a founder of the Society for the Protection of Ancient Buildings, he was determined to work in a way that would respect the original fabric of the medieval castle. True to his word, in the library, which he designed in 1877, he accommodated the unusual existing form of the room—with an overhang to the right—and built shelving and added a gallery. The relief panel above the fireplace by Edward Burne-Jones depicts the Battle of Flodden, and was executed by the sculptor Edgar Boehm. Webb resigned from the work at Naworth in protest of what he saw as unacceptable changes being made to the building. He suggested the Carlisle architect Charles John Ferguson (1840–1904) as his successor.

below left

ROUNTON GRANGE, YORKSHIRE, WAS built by Philip Webb, one of the leading figures of the Arts and Crafts movement, for the industrialist Sir Lowthian Bell in 1873–76. This photograph, taken in 1915, shows the dining room. Above the great dresser against the far wall, also by Webb, is an embroidery of *The Romant de la Rose*, which was designed by William Morris and Burne-Jones, who were friends of the family. It was executed by Lady Bell and her daughter over the course of eight years. *Country Life* described the embroidery as "no less than a historical monument to the greatest decorative movement which modern times have known." It demonstrates the connection between the Arts and Craft movement and the Gothic revival, the Pre-Raphaelites, and an idealization of the medieval past. Rounton Grange was demolished in 1954.

opposite

WIGHTWICK MANOR, OUTSIDE Wolverhampton, was built in 1877–78 by the paint manufacturer Theodore Mander for his wife, Flora. The Manders were keenly interested in the Arts and Crafts movement and employed the timber-frame specialist Edward Ould to construct the house, which takes the form of a medieval timber-frame building. Shown here is a detail of the Oak Room. This photograph was taken in 1996 after the National Trust had restored a partition dividing the bedroom space from its dressing room. The house preserves a remarkable wealth of Morris and Co. furnishings collected by different generations of the family, such as the curtain at far right and the hand-knotted carpet, as well as a collection of Pre-Raphaelite paintings.

left

THE DRAWING ROOM AT STANDEN HOUSE,
West Sussex. Built in 1891–94, Standen was one
of the architect Philip Webb's last houses. It
was built for the Beale family, part of a wealthy
artistic circle in London. The room is simply
finished and without ornamental plasterwork.
Its focus is the fireplace, which is articulated
with an overarch and cross-hatched paneling.
Notice the metal cheeks and fender, made by
John Pearson, of the Guild of Handicraft. He
was also responsible for the drawing room's
copper light fittings. Many other furnishings,
including the superb Morris and Co. carpet,
were introduced in the 1970s. In much of the
house the paneling was painted green. Not
all of the furniture was handmade (the Arts
and Crafts ideal), but was instead supplied by
fashionable London firms.

following pages

PERRYCROFT HOUSE, HEREFORDSHIRE, WAS
built in 1893–94 by C. F. A. Voysey and restored
from 1999 by Mark and Gillian Archer after a
period of institutional use. The drawing room
looks out over the garden through generous
size windows. It is low ceilinged, a reflection
of Voysey's dislike for "the modern craze for
high rooms ... which has led to the destruction
of all effects of repose." He liked simplicity, as
this room, devoid of decorative plaster work,
shows. He also preferred not to paper the walls
with patterns. "We cannot be too simple," he
wrote. "Simplicity requires perfection in all
its details." The fireplace, with its swirling
patterns, is made from Irish Connemara
marble, and the carpet is a modern reweaving
of Voysey's sinuous tulip and rose Donnemara
pattern that was made in Pakistan.

above

THE DINING ROOM AT BLACKWELL, Cumbria, combines a table for meals with an inglenook fireplace for comfortable lounging. Such informal planning, where a single room could have multiple purposes, was typical of the Arts and Crafts. Blackwell was built as a holiday home for a wealthy Manchester brewer and his family by the architect M. H. Baillie Scott between 1898 and 1900. Scott was a worldy figure, and his work, while delighting in the physical qualities of constituent materials and the

handmade, looks beyond Arts and Crafts to the Art Nouveau, a cosmopolitan style that drew inspiration from natural forms. The fireplace is strikingly conceived as an ensemble in blue and white, a variation on the theme of the Delft tiles in its surrounds.

opposite

THE PLEASANCE, GULLANE, SCOTLAND, was built overlooking the links at Muirfield, home of The Honourable Company of Edinburgh Golfers, which opened in 1891.

It was the self-built home of the Scottish architect Sydney Mitchell and was completed between 1897 and 1899. The music room contains a large-scale cycle of decorative plasterwork. Above the fireplace is the Archangel Michael pinioning the devil with his lance and holding the scales of Judgement. Above him on the barrel vault is a delightful frieze of boats on the sea with an abundance of birds and fish. Carried within the various vessels are the Virgin and Child, St. Margaret of Scotland, and a Scottish

king, presumably her consort King Malcolm. The house has been restored since 2012 by the Edinburgh architect Lindsay Buchan.

following pages

A FIREPLACE WITH FLANKING CUPBOARDS at Goddards, Surrey. The house was designed by Edwin Lutyens in 1899 for Frederick and Margaret Mirrielees to provide restful holidays for poor working women (it is now run by the Landmark Trust). The unusual nature of the commission allowed Lutyens, whose work was usually shaped by the exacting demands of the wealthy for modern domestic comforts, to indulge his delight in simplicity. Indeed, the building had no bathrooms or electric light. He wanted "everything of the simplest kind and yet beautiful." In this photograph is an essay in materials with brick, stone, tile, iron, and timber (probably not painted originally), all integrated like pieces in a jigsaw puzzle. When it was finished, Lutyens reported that "the inmates love it & invariably weep when they leave which is comforting."

BARBARA LUTYENS, DAUGHTER OF EDWIN Lutyens, sits at a spinet in the gallery at Lindisfarne Castle, Northumberland. This photograph was taken in 1913 by Charles Lathom, one of *Country Life*'s brilliant early architectural photographers. Lutyens had restored the castle for the founder and proprietor of the magazine, Edward Hudson. This image, which was never published, probably because it was conceived as a portrait of the child, was inspired by the work of such seventeenth-century Dutch painters as Vermeer. The fall of natural light emphasizes the array of surface textures in the room and bestows serenity on the scene. It perfectly illustrates the magazine's Arts and Crafts aesthetic.

IN 1908 EDWIN LUTYENS WAS commissioned to renovate and expand the island castle of Lambay, Co. Dublin, Ireland. This is the head of the stone spiral staircase leading to the extension he built. It is made of blue-grey limestone from the Milverton Quarries at Skerries on the mainland. It was carved with exquisite precision using a professional team of masons employed by the builder Parnell & Sons of Rugby, Warwickshire. A delight in the material of the stone, as well as the value placed upon craftsmanship, are distinguishing marks of the Arts and Crafts aesthetic.

left

A SHOWER AT ARDKINGLAS, ARGYLL,
a house built by Scotland's celebrated Arts
and Crafts architect Robert Lorimer. The
building was commissioned in January 1906
by the industrialist Sir Andrew Noble, who
wanted to eat his dinner in the completed
building on August 1, 1907 (and he did). It
was built in the "Old Scots" style but with
every modern convenience, including
electricity, central heating, a telephone
exchange, fire hoses, Lorimer's patented
lavatories, and this shower, which has wave
and spray controls. Such fittings reflect the
rapidly changing expectations of the wealthy
in Britain, driven in part by the standards of
transatlantic cruise liners.

opposite

VOEWOOD HOUSE, NORFOLK, WAS BUILT
by the architect Edward Schroeder Prior
for the Reverend Percy Lloyd between
1903 and 1905. Shown here is the cloister
room, originally an open loggia, with a
recent mosaic by the Norfolk-based textile
designer Annabel Grey. The patterning
of the original masonry with zig-zag
brickwork and masonry panels expresses
an Arts and Crafts delight in the texture of
materials and color. The house is laid out
on a "butterfly" or "sun-trap" plan, which
aims to make the most of natural light and
air. This type of plan was first devised by
the architect Richard Norman Shaw, Prior's
mentor. Belief in the health-giving benefits
of sunshine, air, and exercise has exerted a
powerful influence on domestic architecture
in the twentieth century.

CHARLESTON FARMHOUSE, SUSSEX, was the home of the artists Duncan Grant and Vanessa Bell from 1916 until their respective deaths in 1961 and 1978. Throughout their lives they adapted the interior, decorating household objects of all kinds. Shown here is the studio of the house, its fireplace painted by Grant in 1928. To the right is a screen created for the opening of the Omega Workshops (1913–19), which were set up by their friend Roger Fry. This produced furniture, fabrics, and household utensils in a "Post-Impressionist" aesthetic of bright colors and bold forms. Fry aimed to blur the distinction between decorative and fine arts. Vanessa Bell was the sister of Virginia Woolf, and this eighteenth-century farmhouse became a retreat for the Bloomsbury Group.

left

CHITCOMBE HOUSE, DORSET, THE HOME OF
Roderick and Lydia Wurfbain, was designed by the
architect Stuart Martin and completed in 2014.
The foyer evokes the "Wrenaissance" architecture
of Edwin Lutyens, but is suffused with an Arts and
Crafts sensibility for materials. The room is paneled
in limed oak and the floor is inlaid with a striking
pattern in Purbeck marble and Portland stone that
hints toward the bold forms of the Art Deco. From
the lobby it is possible to look right through the
dining room to the landscape surrounding the house.
The builder was Shean & Hare and the paneling is by
Mandeville Joinery, both local companies.

below left

A BEDROOM AT ASTHALL MANOR, OXFORDSHIRE.
This house embodies the popular ideal of the
Cotswold manor house, with its grid windows
and rambling plan. It stands in picturesque
relationship to the medieval parish church. This
room, photographed in 2009, has an Arts and Crafts
warmth and simplicity that William Morris would
surely have approved of. Asthall was occupied by the
Mitford family from 1919 until 1926, when this room
served as the family nursery and school room. This
house was one of several that inspired the character
Alconleigh in Nancy Mitford's *The Pursuit of Love*
(1945). The Mitford livery color was indigo blue,
which was used throughout the house.

opposite

THE ENTRANCE HALL OF PAPERHOUSE,
Norfolk. Paperhouse is the self-built home of the
architectural designer Charles Morris. It was
created through the adaptation and extension
of two historic warrener's cottages in the 1980s.
Mr. Morris has been profoundly influenced by the
work of Edwin Lutyens, which he first properly
encountered in a Hayward Gallery exhibition of
1981–82. This hall is dominated by two columns of
Ancaster stone that seem to grow directly from the
floor, like trees in a forest. Facing the front door (to
the left) is a broad window that overlooks the garden.
In the foreground, the interior of the house proper
is demarcated by wooden floor boards and the
tread of the stair. Visible through the far door is the
dining room and kitchen.

following pages

IN 2007, BEN COODE-ADAMS AND FREDDIE
Robins commissioned the architect Anthony
Hudson from Hudson Architects to convert a
disused Tudor barn at Feeringbury, Essex, into
a new home. This view shows the interior of the
barn from the kitchen space. Nearly everything is
recycled, including the two concrete silos across
the room, relics of the agricultural use of this
building in the twentieth century. The silos act as
a screen for the bedrooms on the other side, and
one contains a spiral stair. Mr. Coode-Adams, with
advice from his wife, has done much of the building
work himself. By including salvaged materials, the
disjunction that might naturally exist between new
and old is minimized. The overall result is a building
that might accurately be described as a piece of
Industrial Arts and Crafts.

15

Art Deco

THE ART DECO TAKES ITS NAME FROM THE INTERNATIONAL Exhibition of Modern Decorative and Industrial Arts that was held in Paris in 1925. The name was retroactively bestowed on the style, which was popularized by that exhibition, in 1968. Previously it had been called, simply, Moderne. Art Deco was eclectic in its origins, drawing on Egyptian art and architecture, tribal art from Africa, and even pre-Columbian architecture in Mexico. No less important, it was without a directing ideology, in which respect we shall see that it clearly distinguished itself from the succeeding style of Modernism (though it shares some of its formal characteristics).

If one word might characterize the Art Deco it would have to be electrifying. That's in part because it's the first style to explore the decorative possibilities of electricity and lighting, rather than treat them as functional add-ons. It's also a reference to the mode of expression in the Art Deco, which was one of dazzling contrasts—notably black against white—and shining finishes be they marble, wood veneer, glass, or polished metal. It decisively rejected the organic forms that had characterized Art Nouveau, the style that preceded it, and delighted instead in strong lines, geometric forms, abstract shapes, and bold colors. It signified glamour and opulence. To a striking degree this was a style of consumerism and optimism, a visceral reaction against the horrors and deprivations of World War I.

In Britain Art Deco was predominantly a commercial style particularly associated with urban luxury and high living (including travel). It was popularized in London in such 1930s hotels as the Savoy and the Strand Palace Hotel (demolished in 1969). The capital also included a number of important private houses fitted out in the style. Art Deco country house interiors, however, are a relative rarity. That said, its superficiality and lack of intellectual pretension made it capable of striking combinations with contrasting styles (unlike Modernism). This characteristic made it appealing to those who were seeking conventional grandeur with a modern edge.

The Paris exhibition from which the Art Deco takes its name was one of many international fairs that, after the example of London's Great Exhibition of 1851, played a formative role in the dissemination of ideas across the globe in virtually every field of endeavor from the late nineteenth century onward. They were hugely important occasions for the cities where they were based and, much like the Olympics today, were opportunities to create state-of-the-art architecture and infrastructure for the world to admire. In the early twentieth century their impact was reinforced by the high-quality published photography that was appearing in magazines such as *Life*, *Look*, and *Vanity Fair*, and by 1925 it was possible to promulgate a style around the world, making it both truly international and of the moment. Such was the Art Deco.

previous pages

IN 1930–31 THE ARCHITECT OSWALD Milne created an extension to Claridge's Hotel in London. The new building was in complete contrast to the period interiors that were the staple of luxury hotel design at the time (Claridge's then included Gothic, Louis XVI, and Adam style interiors). The extension was furnished and decorated using English talent, including paintings of trees and foliage by Mary Lea, wall lights by Walter Gilbert, and geometric carpets woven by Wilton to the designs of Marion Dorn. The new bedrooms were enthusiastically described in *Country Life* as "obviously of today and as obviously English." This photograph of a corridor leading to the main reception hall was taken just after the opening of the building but never published.

left

A FRAGMENT FROM A FRIEZE OF Nubians in procession by Glyn Philpot. It formerly graced a 1920s lapis-lazuli dining room—now lost—at Port Lympne, Kent. The architect overseeing the enlargement of the house, Philip Tilden, described the house as "the epitome of all things conducive to luxurious relaxation after the strenuousness of war. It was to be a challenge to the world, telling people that a new culture had risen up from the sick-bed of the old, with new aspirations, eyes upon a new aspect, mind tuned to a new burst of imagination."

opposite

GLEDSTONE HALL, YORKSHIRE, was rebuilt from 1925 by the mill owner Sir Amos Nelson. This photograph of 1935 shows a lobby dominated by the bronze *Au Loup!* (a shepherd urging his hound to chase after a wolf that had slaughtered a sheep) by the French sculptor Louis Auguste Hiolin. This is a Classical interior but one toying with the aesthetic preferences of Art Deco in its highly contrasting bold patterns and reflective surfaces. The predominant use of white in the floors and walls sets off the black in the floor and walls to striking effect. Notice the early electric light fitting with its single disk of clear glass. Curiously, a second version of this picture exists, revealing that the photographer rotated the sculpture for effect.

THE INTERIOR OF ATKINSONS,
a perfume shop at 24 Old Bond Street,
London, which was founded in 1799 and
established at this location in 1832. This
photograph was taken in about 1925. Smart
shop interiors in central London come and
go with extraordinary rapidity, and this
one, after a fire in the twentieth century,
has been entirely rebuilt. Because they
need to capture attention, they often take
styles to extremes and—like clubs, theaters,
and hotels—shop interiors can inspire
domestic imitation. The decorative theme
of this interior was crystal and glass, with
dramatic starburst light fittings and an
inner wall paneled with mirrors. A waterfall
made of crystal cascades down the mirror
against the far wall. The tables have legs in
the form of palm trees, a motif borrowed
from the eighteenth century. Curiously, the
surviving exterior of this opulent building
is Neo-Gothic.

opposite above

THE STUDY AT COLETON FISHACRE,
Devon, built in 1926 for Sir Rupert and
Lady Dorothy D'Oyly Carte. Sir Rupert
reputedly identified the site for the house
from his yacht in 1924. He commissioned
the architect, Oswald Milne, after spotting
his name plaque in the Strand, close to the
Savoy Theatre, which he owned (he was the
son of Gilbert and Sullivan's impresario).
Milne was a pupil of Lutyens, and his Arts
and Crafts sensibilities are apparent here in
the natural finish of the wood. However, in
other rooms the interior tends more overtly
toward the Art Deco; the dining room table,
for example, was made of imitation lapis
lazuli. The playfully illustrated map of the
area and its inset wind dial are signed and
dated "George Spencer Hoffman, 1927."

opposite below

THE DINING ROOM AT ASHCOMBE
Tower, Devon, designed by Brian O'Rorke
in 1934. Used mainly after dark, dining
rooms in the 1930s were inward looking
with furniture and fittings arranged
symmetrically around the central dining
table. Because they were places of
formality, color was important, as was
a conscious sense of theatricality (this
was also a golden age of after-dinner
word games). At Ashcombe the original
chairs remain in place, with pink leather
upholstery, a color echoed in the rag-
rolled walls (a 1980s addition in the spirit
of the original). There is a mirrored side
table bracketed out from the walls, its
frame studded with silver stars, a motif
repeated elsewhere in the room.

above

THE DINING ROOM OF UPMEADS,
Staffordshire, designed by the architect
Edgar Wood in 1908. This room was not
originally paneled, and the wainscoting
was an afterthought in about 1920. At
the end of the room is a fireplace made of
marbles from Siena, Sweden (Swedish
green), and Ireland (Irish moss). The
large grid window was reputedly enlarged
by the owner so that she could enjoy
the garden during breakfast. In many
respects this room is rooted in the Arts
and Crafts, but the building reflects an
awareness of international Modernism.
Industrialization and mass production
encouraged the internationalization of
styles from the late nineteenth century and
underpinned the emergence of Art Deco.

previous pages, left

IN 1926 MR. AND MRS. SAMUEL
Courtauld, celebrated collectors of art, took
a lease on 20 Portman Square, London, a
magnificent late-eighteenth-century town
house. They employed the flamboyant
interior designer Marchese Malacrida,
who first came to England from Como,
Italy, in 1913 as a young cavalry officer, to
help them redecorate the building. This
photograph of Mrs. Courtauld's bathroom
was taken in 1932. The walls are decorated
in semicircular panels of black-and-white
glass, creating a pattern that is bold and

reflective, both qualities beloved in Art
Deco design. The murals on the wall and
ceiling are by John Armstrong, a painter,
illustrator, and set designer with an interest
in Surrealism. They were rediscovered
beneath wallpaper when the bathroom was
recreated in 1997.

previous pages, right

THE SWIMMING POOL OF STOCKGROVE
Park, Bedfordshire, a large country house
built in 1929 by the architect W. Curtis
Green. According to the 1939 description in

Country Life, the barrel vault was painted
"a sea green shade" and the pillars in "dark
green picked out in buff; and the bath itself is
tessellated with small tiles of a peacock blue
colour." The pool formed part of a sports
wing to the house complete with a gun
room and squash court. Sports, especially
squash, and healthy exercise at home,
were becoming increasingly popular in
this period. The clean lines of the detailing
and roof structure, which incorporates a
clerestory of windows in the pitch of the
vault, are typical of Art Deco.

opposite

THE ENTRANCE HALL OF GAYFERE HOUSE, Westminster, in a photograph of 1932. This striking interior, which had just been completed at the time of this photograph, was designed by the architect Oliver Hill in collaboration with the client, Lady Mount Temple. As is typical of Art Deco interiors, it makes striking use of color and contrasts as seen in the steps of alternating black and white marble. There is also an interest in reflective surfaces, including a grid of mirrors on the ceiling (mirrors were similarly used in Lady Mount Temple's

bathroom to astonishing effect), as well as rectilinear forms reminiscent of cubism in the stair rail. The porcelain cats stand like elegant sentries on what are clearly purpose-built plinths integrated within the stair.

above

THE DRAWING ROOM AT MULBERRY House, Westminster. It was one of two rooms—along with a dining room lined in travertine—created by the architect Darcy Braddell for Lady Melchett and completed by 1931, when this photograph

was published. The interiors were inherited from the existing house, which had been designed by Edwin Lutyens around 1910. With the help of two Academicians, the sculptor Charles S. Jagger and painter Glyn Philpot, Braddell created what *Country Life* described in 1931 as "one of the boldest, most complete and original schemes of decoration of our time." The painting depicts the loves of Jupiter (visible here is Leda and the swan) and was executed on silver foil. The fireplace overmantle is of bronze and titled *Scandal*, with gossips ogling two kissing lovers.

A MIRRORED BATHROOM AT NORTH House, Westminster, designed by the architect Oliver Hill for the MP Mr. Robert Hudson and his American wife in a photograph published in 1933. The fluted bath is lined in mosaic, and the ceiling is painted. In the 1920s, encouraged by trans-Atlantic travel on luxury liners, the British discovered the delights of the bathroom. Oliver Hill was one of the leading specialists in these rooms, which were at once private and yet, by virtue of the money lavished upon them, spaces for display. Many of those who commissioned such luxurious bathrooms enjoyed a degree of notoriety in their private lives. This house, along with Gayfere and Mulberry, were all in the immediate neighborhood of Smith Square and were created as part of its fashionable redevelopment between the wars.

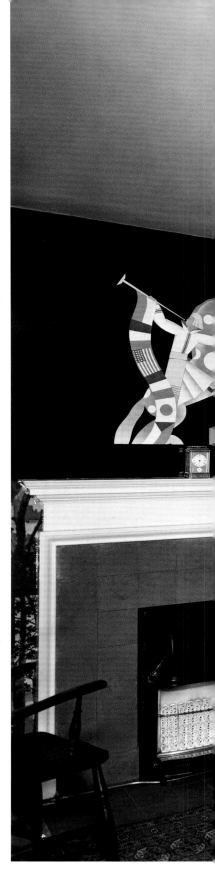

THE SERVANT'S HALL AT 42 CHEYNE
Walk, London, designed by Sir Edwin
Lutyens in 1932 for Guy Liddell, head of
MI5's espionage operations during World
War II, and his wife, Hon. Calypso Baring.
Calypso was the daughter of Cecil and
Maude Baring, who had commissioned
Lutyens to rebuild Lambay Castle on an
island in Dublin Bay. This is a stylish room,
with half of it painted black and the other
half papered with posters. Many of them are
travel posters by Constant Duval, showing
places that would soon be devastated by
war. Over the fireplace is the stylized figure

of a trumpeter on a rearing horse holding a
banner composed of international flags. It's
not quite clear what the significance of this
display was. This photograph was published
in 1933.

left

THE NAUTICAL COCKTAIL BAR AT THE Ladies Carlton Club, Grosvenor Place, London, photographed in 1936 shortly after it was built. According to *Country Life*, this room was separated from the dining room by "that magical kind of mirror that is transparent or reflective according to whether there is illumination behind it or not." Evidently, the two rooms could be made intervisible. The design of the room as a ship was suggested to its architect, Darcy Braddell, by preexisting structural girders, which were incorporated and painted "lacquer red." The bar was made of Indian laurel banded with pewter, and electric lighting was provided through the portholes. In an age of travel by luxury liners, a bar with Art Deco touches suggested both comfort and modernity.

below left

THE MORNING ROOM AT CHARTERS, Sunningdales, a large Art Deco house created for the rich industrialist Frank Parkinson by the architects Adie, Button and Partners. *Country Life* covered the house in 1944 and described the pictures by Adrian Daintrey—of the riverside, an outdoor café, and Pimlico street—as being integral to the design of the room. The description goes on to note the "squarish forms" of the furniture and asserts that the photograph, "if looked at abstractedly, makes patterns recalling cubist designs." As is typical of Art Deco, the surfaces are striking and often reflective, including the black marble fireplace and the Australian Walnut cabinet. The textiles were in "quiet brown or greenish weaves."

opposite

THE MAIN SALOON OF THE MALAHNE, a yacht commissioned in 1937 by William "Bill" Lawrence Stephenson, the chairman of Woolworths from 1931. He used it for business visits to America, as well as for recreation. The yacht had an eventful war, even serving in the evacuation from Dunkirk, and underwent many internal adaptations. She has been completely restored since 2009. Rather than faithfully recreating the lost original interiors of the vessel, the interior designer Guy Oliver of Oliver Laws has reinvented them in a 1930s idiom. Dividing the saloon from the main stairs and a spacious sun deck is an elegant lattice of glass, metal, and painted panels. Concealed by the screen is an ingeniously designed games table by Jerome Cordie.

THE ENTRANCE HALL AT ELTHAM PALACE, Kent, photographed in 1999, following its restoration and refurnishing by English Heritage. In the 1930s the house was purchased and restored by Stephen and Virginia Courtauld. They created interiors in many different styles involving different designers. The hall, with its shallow dome, was the work of Swedish architect Rolf Engströmer. It is lined with wood paneling covered with intarsia decoration. To either side of the entrance are depictions and personifications of Venice and Stockholm. The juxtaposition of northern and southern civilizations may be drawn from the depressing analysis of Oswald Spengler's *The Decline of the West* (1918). *Country Life* photographs taken in 1937 were used to recreate the lost original furnishings. Neil Stevenson made the replica table and Marion Dorn the rug.

16

Modern

& Post-Modern

DESPITE ITS NAME, MODERNISM IS NOW ITSELF A HISTORIC style that first emerged more than a century ago. The style's roots are in new technology and the possibilities created by mass production, and it found its catalyst in the calamities of World War I. It was pioneered in central Europe and America and arrived relatively late to Britain, though it had harbingers in some of the aesthetic preferences of the Art Deco.

Like the Arts and Crafts movement, Modernism has at its heart a laudable utopian ideal: that industrialization had at last made good design, whether in architecture or furniture or tableware, accessible to everyone, rich and poor alike. Its central aesthetic dogma was that function should dictate form. Expressed another way, beauty was a quality expressed through purpose rather than craftsmanship. The house should be—in the famous phrase of the architect Le Corbusier, a leading exponent of Modernism—"a machine for living." Architecture was transformed from an art to a science.

The British architectural establishment in the 1930s accepted the ideal of Modernism but rejected its dogma. For that reason, between the world wars, many shared the hope of *Country Life*'s architectural editor, Christopher Hussey, that Modernism would be inculcated within Britain's existing architectural tradition. That this never happened was in part a consequence of World War II.

In intellectual terms the war lent credibility to the idea that the modern world needed to break free from its past. That meant that Modernism, which claimed to express contemporary needs and desires, seemed to represent the future. The practicalities of reconstruction after the war, however, also favored a style that permitted the erection of houses in large numbers and on the same principles as every other kind of utilitarian architecture, from factories and hospitals to airports and warehouses.

Industrialization had a profound effect on the British domestic interior. Among other changes, it permitted the mass production of plate glass, which allowed whole walls of glass to be created relatively cheaply. Whereas Art Deco had explored the reflective or decorative qualities of glass, as for example in mirrors and lamps, Modernists were fascinated with natural light and clear windows that brought the outdoors into the home.

The creation of large windows in turn depended upon another innovation: the reduction of structure. The use of girders and concrete made possible the erection of ever larger flat, structural spans. It became possible, in fact, to create modular buildings essentially built up from skeletal cubes (it's no coincidence that the birth of Modernism coincided with Cubism). As the structure of buildings became ever more simplified, so was it possible to open out external walls to the maximum and set them with windows. No less important, it also permitted the interiors of buildings to communicate more freely and openly with one another. Infilling materials, meanwhile, became essentially cosmetic, so it was a matter of choice whether you created walls of bricks, breeze blocks, or glass.

The advent of open-plan living coincided with another revolution in British life: the decline of domestic service. Without servants hovering about, integrated living interiors became more desirable. So too did smaller rooms, which were more comfortable and affordable to heat and light. At the same time, new appliances that simplified life, such as the Hoover vacuum cleaner, washing machine, and refrigerator, became widely available. The culminating outcome of this change has been the multiuse daytime interior: the kitchen-living-dining room.

Just as Modernism simplified the architecture of the domestic interior, so did it react against clutter. As the structure of buildings had been reduced, so too was that of furniture. Wood, moreover, now became only one of many materials used to make it. After the example of Le Corbusier, meanwhile, some Modernists applied theories of color to their designs, distinguishing between the visual effects of those artificially derived from the spectrum and natural color. As the complement to the truly functional interior, however, from the late 1920s, white (or off-white) overwhelmingly became the color of choice on the walls of all rooms in the home.

previous pages
THE ROUND ROOM OF PORT ELIOT, Cornwall, was the creation of the Regency architect Sir John Soane in 1804–6. In 1988, when he inherited the house, the 10th Earl of St. Germans cleared the room of clutter and commissioned the artist Robert Lenkiewicz to create this giant mural. After thirty years of intermittent work, the painting remains incomplete. It depicts the Condition of Man and such themes as death, decay, loneliness, love, passion, friendship, and hope. The painting is in complete contrast to the style of the room, yet as a panorama it reinforces the logic of the space. A playful interrelationship between the contemporary and the historic is a recurrent theme of Post-Modern interiors in country houses.

The technical innovations of Modernism—modular construction and large glass windows—remain living traditions in contemporary architecture. So too have some of its aesthetic choices, namely conformity and simplicity. Yet the design of domestic spaces in this idiom has undergone changes and variations. One of the most important in recent years is the attempt to give buildings a distinct character and to play down the very quality—industrialization—that underpinned the first development of the style. For simplicity, I would characterize such developments stylistically as Post-Modern.

One theme of Post-Modernism has been to cheer up the relative austerity of the industrial interior. This can be achieved through the use of color, quirky detail, or reference to locality. In some cases Modernist buildings deliberately cannibalize existing structures, creating contemporary homes with a visual depth of history.

Another theme of Post-Modernism has been an interest in environmentally friendly architecture. In the main this concern has been a technical one and correspondingly invisible. Nevertheless, it has brought about the reintroduction of timber to interiors, a material that ideologues in the 1920s would have viewed with suspicion.

Post-Modernism is a revolution from within the mainstream of Modernism born of a desire to be innovative. As this book shows, however, there are patrons and architects working today who have completely different perspectives on style. In this regard, it's common in popular debate to distinguish between architecture that is contemporary and that which is historically inspired (its critics call it "pastiche"). These two modes, it is argued, respectively use contemporary and historic materials, steel as opposed to stone or glass fascia instead of brickwork and sashes.

To my mind, however, this debate is as false as it is unhelpful. Post-Modern and "traditional" architects, as they generally describe themselves, are both struggling with a common problem: how do you personalize and contextualize architecture today? As this book powerfully illustrates, in their various ways and according to different tastes, both groups continue to achieve this in fascinating and inventive ways. Moreover, to focus on the achievements of one or the other group would be to present a distorted view of what's going on in the world of interior design at the present moment.

That is not, perhaps, a conventional comment. The coverage of interior design in most magazines and books today, for example, is fixated on what is new. *Country Life*'s approach is different. That's partly because, as a result of its Arts and Crafts roots, the magazine is less interested in novelty or style than in something beyond either: objects of quality and beauty, particularly the handmade. It's also because in Britain and Ireland, we live with an extraordinary quantity and quality of inherited buildings. These are not only marvelous and fascinating in their own right, redolent of history, but an ongoing challenge to their owners, because for them to remain in use and to survive in the present, each new generation must make them livable in their own style and times.

In this regard, indeed, the oldest and grandest of houses are not only the work of those who created them, but of everyone who has used and cherished them since. By the same token, they also remain in some sense quite as contemporary as a room newly designed and furnished today. So to see Modernism and Post-Modernism as the concluding episodes—for the present—of a linear narrative would be mistaken. The contemporary world of style is represented not just by this concluding chapter, but by the whole of this book. And the good news is, therefore, that, whatever happens in the next chapter, the vocabulary of contemporary interior style promises only to continue to grow and expand.

above

OPEN-PLAN LIVING: A VIEW FROM THE
central octagonal dining hall of Yaffle Hill,
Dorset, into the Big Room, or drawing room.
The interior is marvelously light due to its
huge windows made by Crittall, a maker of
steel-framed windows. The dining room
is described as having "cream walls, grey
silk curtains, and a chromium steel table."
Yaffle Hill was designed by Edward Maufe
for a director of the former Poole Pottery
and published by *Country Life* in 1933 to
coincide with the opening of the British
Industrial Art Exhibition held at Dorland
Hall in London. In the judgement of the
magazine the interiors demonstrated that
Modernism could be national (not just
international), that industrial art could
also be fine art, and that function did not
necessarily have to determine the form.

opposite

THE ENTRANCE GALLERY OF BROOK HOUSE,
London, in 1939. This two-story penthouse was
created for Lord and Lady Louis Mountbatten
by the architect Leonard Rome Guthrie and
the New York decorator Mrs. Cosden. It was
entered by a lift, "the fastest outside America,"
according to the admiring description in
Country Life. The interior celebrated travel.
Lord Mountbatten's rooms were furnished in
the manner of a ship's cabin, and his study was
dominated by a relief map of the world. Such
glamorous décor merely set off to advantage
the family portraits and antique furniture
that proclaimed the couple's aristocratic
connections. The gallery ran the full width
of the property and divided the formal rooms
overlooking Hyde Park from the services. In
the photograph, the ceiling appears to be gilded
or silvered.

following pages

THE HALL OF GRIBLOCH, STIRLING-
shire, a house designed for John and Helen
Colville by the architect Basil Spence
in 1937. Its great bow window enjoys a
spectacular view and also receives light
reflected from the outdoor swimming
pool. The furnishings of the house, shown
in this photograph of 1998, are largely
original. The designer, John Hill of Green
and Abbot, created a maritime theme for
the room: the sea-like palette of light blue,
turquoise, and mauve; the rope and cockle-
shell cornice (just visible to the right); the
shell chairs; and the shell carpet. The stair,
however, was designed by the Parisian
metalworker Raymond Subes; its railing
was made by the Edinburgh firm Charles
Henshaw Ltd. The glass and chrome
chandelier is by Betty Joel.

THE MAIN STAIR OF BIRCHENS
Spring, Buckinghamshire, designed
by the architect John Campbell in
the 1930s and photographed in 1938.
It comprises a series of monumental
arches executed with Modernist
minimalism and painted in white.
The steps are decorated with marble-
inlay, a detail presumably borrowed
from Roman architecture. Campbell
studied and worked in central Europe
and Italy, eventually establishing
himself as a professor of architecture
at Munich. *Country Life* admired
his ability to reinvent traditional
architectural forms to dynamic new
effect. He used a standard, cubic
measurement as a means of creating
visual coherence between spaces: at
Birchens Spring the measurement is a
seven-foot cube.

THE LIVING ROOM AT BENTLEY
Wood, East Sussex, the self-built
home of the Russian-born architect
Serge Chermayeff, photographed
in 1939. Light floods in from the
enormous floor-to-ceiling windows
to the right, which also offer superb
views and bring the outdoors into the
house. A line of rectangular flagstones
runs along the right side of the room,
further linking the interior with the
exterior. Chermayeff commissioned
art for the property from both the
painter John Piper and the sculptor
Henry Moore (for the garden). The
house was so radical in form that it
was denied permission by the local
building authority at the first attempt.

previous pages

THE LIBRARY OF RED HOUSE, SUFFOLK, the home of composer Benjamin Britten and the singer Peter Pears. It was completed in 1964 to designs by the architect Peter Collymore. The room was intended for different usages, including musical events, meetings, and quiet reading. The division of space is accentuated by a central row of timber uprights running down its middle (not visible). A pine ceiling and quarry-tile floor lend warmth to the interior. This corner of the room, with its narrow floor-to-ceiling window allowing light to shine in, is intended for reading. As seen around the fireplace, its walls are covered in Japanese gold wallpaper imitating tiles. The pronounced structural elements and shelves are painted uniform white, Modernism's color of choice.

below

A BEDROOM AT TURN END, BUCKING-hamshire, one of a group of three houses—including The Turn and Middle Turn—designed by Peter Adlington in the 1960s. The sliding door in one wall opens the room into a garden enclosed by a pre-existing wall. That wall also defines the far end of the bedroom and, by the placement of potted plants against it, creates the impression that the garden has entered the building. It's an illusion reinforced by the tile floor extending from the interior out to the garden. The room has an industrial simplicity with its painted breeze (or screen) blocks, but the varnished pine wood adds warmth and a sense of intimacy. The bed also has a base of breeze blocks.

opposite

THE MASTER BEDROOM OF TANCREDS FORD, Surrey, designed by Roderick Gradidge in the early 1980s. It's an essay in reflection: there are mirrors extending around much of the interior, including the ceiling, the tables, and the cupboards. Circular convex mirrors just visible at each corner of the room are an unexpected reference to the work of the regency architect Sir John Soane. Lights are set inside the outer strip of the ceiling, which is fixed with two-way blue mirrors. The wardrobe is also covered in mirrors and the mirror balls to either side of the bed are floor lamps.

opposite

IN 1960 THE INTERIOR DESIGNER, DAVID Hicks, and his wife, Lady Pamela, bought Britwell Salome, an eighteenth-century country house in Oxfordshire. This photograph, published in 1972, shows the drawing room as they redecorated it. It reflects Hicks's interest in combining the historic—for example, the fireplace (not an original fixture in the room) and the painted French furniture—with the modern. Particularly striking is this regard is the scroll-top painting over the fireplace, specially commissioned from the artist Bruce Tippett, and the carpet. The cool palette of the room is enlivened by the careful use of pattern and splashes of bright color. There are striking collections of objects gathered in the room, what Hicks described as "tablescapes."

above

BRIGHT, COLORFUL AND ZANY, FARRS House, Wiltshire, is a perfect example of Post-Modernism. It's the home of the furniture designer John Makepeace, and the dining room contains furniture made by him, including the table with arched supports (so that no one at the table has to straddle a leg) and its chairs, each unique and representing a particular commission; the one nearest the camera has a striking finish in stripes of yew and bog oak. The fish was carved by Howard Raybould, and a grey-patinated bronze stack of cloud-like forms to the right of the fireplace, *Level Head*, is by Tony Cragg. Among the paintings on the wall is Kevin Sinnott's *The Runner* (at left). Another painting inspired the Tracy Oldfield carpet, which was designed locally and made in Yorkshire by a needle-punch technique.

THE DRAWING ROOM OF 45, THE PARK, in Cheltenham. The house is a modern villa designed by the architect Hugh Petter in collaboration with the owner of the house, Toby Roberts. The Neo-Classical style of the villa reflects a desire to fit politely within the streets of this attractive Regency town. It's also expressed in the choice of furniture, which incorporates several Georgian pieces. The house, however, is also consciously modern, as seen in the gas fireplace that is raised within the wall. Another interesting feature is the skylight to the right of the room over the mahogany cabinet. The asymmetric placement of natural light sources is found in some Modernist interiors.

THE HALL OF DOWNLEY HOUSE, Hampshire, designed by the architectural practice Birds Portchmouth Russum. It runs through the full width of the house and has a glass door at either end, allowing the room to be opened onto the garden. The builders of the house, Mr. and Mrs. Chris Taee, are wine connoisseurs who were working in the trade when they first met. So the design of the hall is inspired by the giant oak barrels known as *foudres* that are used in winemaking and are capable of holding 600 liters (132 gallons) each. The horizontal beams and square window at the far end echo the form of the ribs bracing the ends of the barrel. The hoops are made from laminated timber.

opposite

THE KITCHEN OF COOMBE LODGE, Berkshire, a new house designed by the architect Ptolemy Dean and commissioned in 2006. This family room by Jane Taylor is in complete contrast to the formal interiors of the house, which are designed and decorated in the spirit of Regency. Natural boards on the floor complement the oatmeal-white that covers the interior and its furnishings. The shelving visually extends the structural grid of the ceiling to the floor. It also turns the far wall into a display case, framing varied contents as a collage or still-life. This light and airy aesthetic is Scandinavian in origin. The French windows to the left open onto a small terrace and garden, and there are long views through the far window.

below

IN JUNE 2008 A SCULPTURE PARK, named Jupiter Artland, opened in the grounds of Bonnington House, Edinburgh, the home of Mr. and Mrs. Robert Wilson. The park possesses a remarkable collection of sculpture by contemporary artists. This refreshment caravan complements the character of the park itself, being at once stridently contemporary—with its stainless steel table and dramatic terminating half-dome of shiny steel—and yet playful with brilliant pink leather cushions. Confident absurdity is one of the most engaging qualities of Post-Modernism. It is also one of the most disarming, because it inevitably sounds a bit pompous to criticize the absurd in earnest.

following pages

THE FORMER DINING ROOM OF Chinthurst Hill, Surrey, the first country house of the young architect Edwin Lutyens that was built from 1893. This photograph of 2015 shows the house after the completion of its restoration by the gallery owner Anna Hunter, which began in 1999. She reunited the property, which had been divided up, and furnished much of it with period furniture. This room, however, has a contemporary look and feel and illustrates how furnishings can transform the aesthetics of a well-proportioned Victorian room. The light fittings and carpet evoke Modernist designs of the 1930s.

left

THE VIEW FROM THE POOL HOUSE AT Stockton House, Wiltshire, completed in 2017. It looks toward the Tudor manor house that it serves, recently restored by the architect Lucy Barron of Donald Insall Associates and the contractor R. Moulding and Co. The pool is situated in what had been a carp pond and is discretely concealed behind a historic wall and a yew hedge. As a building primarily designed for use in warmer weather, the glazed front facing the pool can be opened out, as shown here. There are large skylights to make the interior as bright as possible. Between the pool and the house is a wide stone terrace for sunbathing.

following pages

THE ANNEX OF FLINT HOUSE ON THE Waddesdon estate, Buckinghamshire, a freestanding building that reproduces on a smaller scale the forms of the main house immediately aligned with it. The new building, which was completed in 2015 and designed by Skene Catling de la Peña, is open plan, with a first-floor bedroom and balcony connected by a stair to a kitchen and living room below. A small sunken patio visible in the distance opens onto the fields beyond. Glass plays an important role in the interior, opening out the space visually—in the case of the stair rail—as well as relating it to the outside world. Flint House garnered numerous awards, including RIBA House of the Year in 2015.

THE DINING TABLE OF CARING WOOD,
Kent, enjoys magnificent views over the
countryside. To the left, the window seems
to frame the scene like a living picture on
the wall. The table stands on one side of
an open-plan dining room and kitchen, the
most important in a series of living rooms
that constitute the core of this country house
designed by architects James Macdonald
Wright and Niall Maxwell. Opening off these
central living spaces are four independent
cottages, each one available for members
of the extended family that commissioned
the building. There are openings cut into
the walls and ceiling that create vistas right
through the house and also create pools of
light within it. The house won the 2017 RIBA
House of the Year Award.

Acknowledgments

I AM DEEPLY INDEBTED TO ALL THOSE WHO HAVE MADE the production of this book both possible and pleasurable. First, there is the small circle of writers who contribute regularly to the architectural pages of *Country Life*, including Clive Aslet, Nicholas Cooper, Michael Hall, Jeremy Musson, Alan Powers, John Martin Robinson, Geoffrey Tyack, Roger White, and the late Gavin Stamp. Many of the book's insights—though none of its errors—come from them and also from the many owners and curators of the houses who have so generously helped the magazine to record the properties in their possession and care. No less important has been the work of the photographers, particularly Paul Highnam and Will Pryce and the late Paul Barker. The hard work they have put in over many years helps make this book as beautiful as it is. Then there is the team that actually produce the magazine each week, particularly the subs who at different times have worked on the architectural pages and purged them (and therefore this book) of errors: Octavia Pollock, Annunciata Walton, and James Fisher. Also, I must thank my colleagues Giles Kime and Mary Miers for their insights and help. The magazine's editor, Mark Hedges, has supported this project and the small and efficient team who manage the *Country Life* archive—Sarah Hart, Paula Fahey, and Melanie Bryan—have worked hard and cheerfully to make its riches available. Finally, I'm very grateful to Charles Miers, publisher of Rizzoli International Publications, for commissioning this book, to Andrea Danese for editing it, and to Robert Dalrymple for its design. JG

Index

ENDPAPERS
The pattern Frognal, made by
Hamilton Weston Wallpapers, is a
design dating from about 1760.

First published in the United States of America
in 2019 by Rizzoli International Publications, Inc.
300 Park Avenue South, New York, NY 10010

www.rizzoliusa.com

Publisher: Charles Miers
Editor: Andrea Danese
Design: Robert Dalrymple
Production Manager: Kaija Markoe
Rights and Permissions: *Country Life*
Managing Editor: Lynn Scrabis

Typeset in Sentinel and Grot10
Printed in Italy

2019 2020 2021 2022 / 10 9 8 7 6 5 4 3 2 1

ISBN: 978-0-8478-6551-2

Visit us online:
Facebook.com/RizzoliNewYork
Twitter: @Rizzoli_Books
Instagram.com/RizzoliBooks
Pinterest.com/RizzoliBooks
Youtube.com/user/RizzoliNY
Issuu.com/Rizzoli

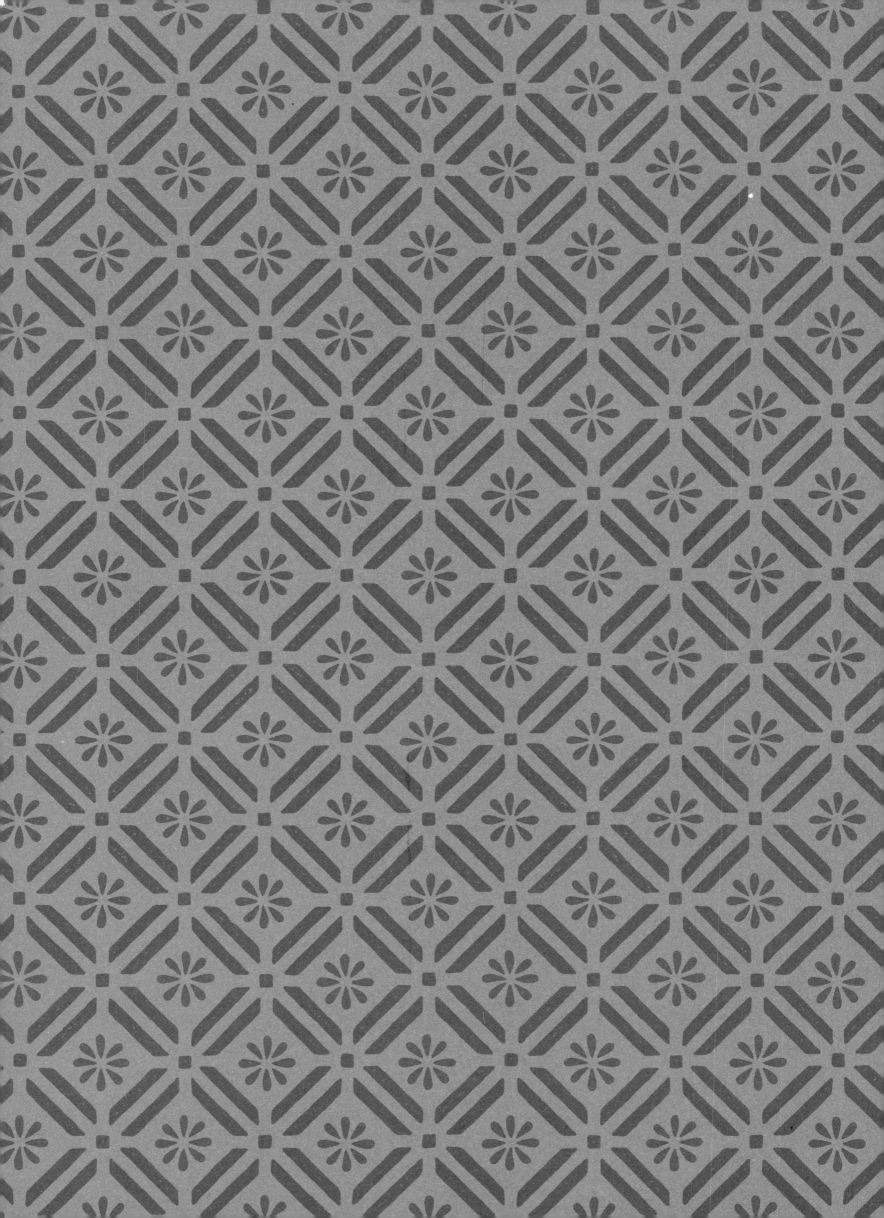